ISSUES
IN YOUR
TISSUES

HOW TO NAVIGATE LIFE THROUGH YOUR BODY'S MESSAGING

ANGEL HOWARD

BRIGHTRAY
PUBLISHING®

We help busy professionals write and publish their stories
to distinguish themselves and their brands.

(407) 287-5700 | Winter Park, FL
info@BrightRay.com | www.BrightRay.com

ISBN: 978-1-956464-53-5

Published in the United States of America.
BrightRay Publishing ® 2024

PRAISE FOR
ISSUES IN YOUR TISSUES

We personally benefited from Angel's movement classes and are thrilled to see her share her somatic work with the world. She somehow has centuries of wisdom in one lifetime! Highly recommend!

– Drs. Edward and Dorothy Kendall, MD

Issues in Your Tissues *is a transformative exploration of self-guided healing, offering readers a profound understanding of somatic movement. Howard's brilliant approach to bodily awareness and movement provides a pathway to deep emotional and physical healing. It is not just informative but also deeply compassionate, making* Issues in Your Tissues *a valuable addition to the field of self-care literature.*

– Ed Bolden-Greer, Founder of
Arbor College - School of Massage

For anyone who has been ignoring their intuition and "gut" for too long—this book is for you. Not only is Angel Howard honest and vulnerable about her own journey, but she offers real guidance on how to work through the trauma we all carry through somatic movement to arrive at a place of peace, power, and presence.

– Catherine Porth, Founder of
Let Her Speak

Issues in Your Tissues offers a holistic approach to self-discovery and healing through the ChakraMental Method™. With its insightful reflections and practical exercises, this book empowers readers to reconnect with their bodies, emotions, and inner elements, providing a transformative journey toward balance and empowerment.

– Dr. Laura Cole, Author of
New Thoughts Create a New Life

I'm amazed at how, with grace and humor, Angel presents a fun way to find real happiness and joy. She simply reveals the "whoo-hoo!" that's inside us all!

– Kelly Searle, Author of
The Naked Executive

Angel does a great job of striking a balance of being vulnerable while being diplomatic. It's truly a great read and an amazing resource.

– Allison Kelly, Chief Creative
Consultant for AK Creative

To Mom,

*Thank you for the freedom
to dance.*

TABLE OF CONTENTS

 **FOREWORD**

"The body always remembers what you're trying to forget" is a phrase that I have become known for in my work with clients and students, in speaking engagements, and in my books. I came to understand this concept intimately, deeply, and completely through the blistering wake-up call of over a dozen illnesses that confined me to bed for weeks at a time and put me on over nine pharmaceutical drugs that only made me sicker. I was in my twenties, but my body felt 80 years old. It would take nearly a decade to find the pathway to healing. Meanwhile, I suffered.

My path would lead me to discover the link between the awful childhood abuse I endured and how my body stored those experiences. I would learn firsthand that emotional stress and negative beliefs can drain the body of its precious energy, which would eventually affect my biology. I would also come to learn that intuition would lead me out of that immense pain and into true and lasting healing.

The body sends us signals—emotional messengers from the past that create opportunities for us to transmute them in the present. But to do this, we must first listen to the body and decode the messages it has been holding for us in the form of aches, pains, and illnesses. Sometimes, the pain has not surfaced yet—rather, the body awaits our participation in releasing the emotional hurt. If only we would take up that mantle.

Angel Howard has explored these concepts from the inside out for over three decades. Her willingness to get raw and vulnerable by sharing her own traumas and transformation is powerful. It helps us all see that we are not alone in our pain, and the way through it isn't to talk about our stories until we feel like we are spinning in them with no end in sight. While talk therapy is an incredible beginning to healing, there is so much more than that. The body holds the keys.

In *Issues in Your Tissues*, Angel helps readers witness their own bodies as keepers of the past. She has created a system of healing that weaves together ancient wisdom, the glory of nature, and the infinite intelligence that each person has within them. This work is a guidebook into you, precious you, that allows you to have realizations and begin healing just by reading Angel's words. Whether you have recently discovered the wisdom of your body or you've been exploring somatic therapies for many years, Angel has the ability to meet you where you are and help you go from there using the processes she has created and tested for decades.

Today, there is an explosion of somatic therapies and body awareness. There are thousands of newcomers to the field who may grasp the concepts but have had little applied experience. As one of the pioneers in somatic healing, Angel has blazed a trail for the seekers of today. She is deeply loving, generous, and committed to growth not only in her role as a practitioner but also as a mother, partner, and friend. She is at once soft and fierce with a bold and brave heart that makes her take risks that I personally marvel at. Whether she's swinging on a trapeze, walking over hot coals, spinning in aerial silks, or dancing in harmonious flow, she brings power and strength to everything she does. It is a thing of beauty to witness.

I find that a key element missing in many somatic therapies today is something Angel has in spades—a deep understanding of the impossibility of making somatic healing a solely intellectual and logical pursuit. If the energetic and spiritual components are missing, then the essence is lost. Angel achieves this through her use of the elements of nature as well as the connection to intuition, which is the current of spirit. In this way, her book offers a truly holistic perspective that is very easily understood and can be applied to your daily life.

As you read, I encourage you to reflect on your own stories of loss and pain and see them as your personal guide toward healing just as Angel communicates her own experience. Then, connect with the special way Angel has of bringing you toward the light by using the body as an instrument of transmutation. Read this book with those eyes, and you will experience powerful healing. Let her truth lead you to find your own.

– Dr. Meg Haworth, PhD
Transpersonal Psychologist

MOVE YOUR BODY

After a long day at work, school, or even home, have you ever felt like your body has become stagnant? Are you even aware of the physical component of you? Do you pay attention to your body when it's stiff, achy, and sluggish? No? Well, stop and take note of your framework—your hardware, so to speak—that houses your mental and emotional software.

When you feel something, your body reveals its message to you. You don't have to listen to it, all the pain and the tension. You can ignore it. But not only will it *persist*, it will *escalate* until you take action. So, listen. Listen and then express its message. Let it all out. Move! Shrug your shoulders, shake every part of your body, and shudder like an earthquake. Get your blood flowing, shake your bones, squeeze and release your muscles. Now, how does that feel?

Your body has been a constant partner in your life, storing your experiences, thoughts, and feelings since you were in the womb. Any trauma that happens to you, around you, or in you will imprint and shape how you respond to your environment, both internally and externally. Your corpus, your chassis, your *body* is communicating with you all the time. The secret to a happier and more fulfilling life lies deep in your tissues. Are you listening?

Issues in Your Tissues is a book about this conversation, a guide to understanding your body's messages through what's called somatic movement, the process by which you can begin listening, interpreting, and self-correcting. You will no longer be a victim of your negative thoughts, painful memories, and body dysmorphia! Instead, you can start speaking the same language as your body.

This is a skill: learning to ask and answer questions about what brings you pain, sadness, and anxiety. That's the intention behind *Issues in Your Tissues*—to teach you this skill so that you can both diagnose and navigate your way around discomfort and trauma.

By the end of this journey toward self-truth, you will be reconnected with your body, feeling free and light as though a 1,000-pound weight has been pulled off of your chest. Most importantly, you will understand how to claim a more vivacious and vibrant life, whatever that may look like for you. I hope this book can be your wayfinder toward that life, toward that self-love, and toward that feeling of fun, sexiness, and happiness. All of it lies here, in your tissues.

So, where to begin? Think back. *All* the way back—to your childhood and how you expressed your feelings then.

I, for example, was a wild child. Barefoot in the grass, I would dance in the woods near my home and imagine I was entertaining fairies and elves. An abandoned stone fire pit was my kitchen, and all the trees and flowers were magical, dancing along with me as they shook their branches and leaves in the wind. Even back then, dance was an outlet, my daily escape. I could express my thoughts and feelings, everything I couldn't put into words, through creative and spontaneous movement. We have all been children, so we remember how intense and confusing it is to figure out who we are in our personal and public environments. As a child, these emotions intensified in my body. But I innately knew I had to shake them off to stop their ripple effect in my life.

I started dancing at the age of three. My parents would ask me to entertain their friends at parties, and I would dance on my tiptoes, leaping in the air or diving into a cartwheel, always ending my performance with a bow for their applause. I took my first dance class at 14—modern dance, the least rigid of most disciplines. I threw all my adolescent angst into the movements. I then performed, choreographed, and produced several dance programs for the following 10 years while also competing, at one time or another, in six different sports. I relied on my body. I trusted my body. I remained loyal to this vessel and could not escape it no matter how much pain it expressed.

Even though dance was my outlet, my love interest was psychology. My pursuit of understanding the human mind and its integral connection to our physical and emotional states drew me into the world of neuroplasticity, neuro-linguistic programming, and mind-body modalities to re-pattern learned behavior, negative thoughts, and self-sabotage. Basically, I learned how to give the controls back to the human inside the body for self-correction and navigation.

This is where dance, movement, and psychology merged to become somatic movement therapy. Amanda Baker, the director of the Center for Anxiety and Traumatic Stress Disorders and a clinical psychologist in the Department of Psychiatry at Massachusetts General Hospital, defines somatic therapy as "a treatment focusing on the body and how emotions appear within the body. Somatic therapies posit that our body holds and expresses experiences and emotions, and traumatic events or unresolved emotional issues can become 'trapped' inside."[1]

As the title of Dr. John Gray's book, *What You Feel, You Can Heal*, suggests, allowing your body to feel and express what is compressed is the first step to healing and regaining control over your body, thoughts, actions, and reactions. Without letting it all out—whether through crying, screaming, dancing, writing, or any other form of expression—your feelings and experiences will instead sink deep into your tissues and bones. And once your trauma is wedged in deep enough, it takes over control. You cannot let that happen. So, no matter how tough it gets, you must fight for your life, for control over yourself, and for your well-being and body. After all, it belongs to you and you alone, not your past.

Flash forward to the present: I still dance, but now *with* people as I teach them how to get out of their minds and into their bodies. I show them how to release and stabilize, how to be flexible and focused, and most importantly, how to love themselves genuinely. I have helped thousands exude confidence through body language, heal their traumas through expression, and build themselves up again by practicing conscious movement to self-correct and thrive.

I call this beautiful mix of body psychology and art—because dance *is* art—the ChakraMental Method™. Now, when I coach clients, I try to help them return to these innate, wonderlike instincts they've had since childhood and channel their body movements into something unimaginable. There's such an incredible capacity for healing in ourselves; we just need to get out of our minds and into our bodies to find it.

You can probably guess the main component of this method: expression. But to express, you need to listen to the pit in your stomach, the squeeze in your heart, the feeling within you that pulls you in a certain direction.

Ask it, "What are you telling me?" Listen to its message and heed it. Do *not* argue with it, discount it, or squash it because our *bodies don't lie!*

Something needs your attention. Accept it. Express it, give it a voice, let it move through you with a shiver, a melting motion, a brisk walk, or an all-out sprint. Maybe you have to express it one time. Maybe it takes a few times or even 100 times. But who cares how long it takes? Just get it out! Only then will you have an opening to connect back with what's truly yours.

No trauma has ever been solved by just thinking about it really hard, no matter how convenient that would be. Instead, by choosing expression and movement, you stand in defiance and say, "No, I'm not going to ignore it and run away. I'm going to move it through me. I'm going to allow it—the trauma, the emotion, the shadow—to be there." Accepting what is hidden in our tissues is one of the scariest steps you will ever take in your life. It won't be easy, but you have to give it space, acknowledge its existence, and allow it to be okay. Embrace it, feel it, express it, and let it go.

It was probably my love for accomplishing physical goals in sports that made me feel comfortable and present in my body. My mother said she always knew what type of day I had at school by the way I walked home from the bus stop. Here's a public relations hack: people in our environments are reading our hidden stories through our body language all the time. I am told that when I walk into a room or up on a stage, I exude a confidence that puts people at ease. When I speak to an audience live or on a camera, my shoulders are supported, my rib cage is lifted up and off my pelvis, my chest is relaxed, and my movements are intentional. More than anything, I am *present* and conscious as a whole person, mentally, physically, and emotionally aligned. What you see, hear, and feel is what you get—no hidden messages, no sneaky negative stories being told by my body while my voice speaks of positivity. But the only reason I'm able to do this is because I've learned the art of integrating my mind and body. I am one. I am whole, no matter where I go or what I do. And now, I'm writing this book to help you achieve this harmony too, through an expressive art form I know best: dance movement.

Before you start to expect a one-two-three-four choreography within this book, stop. In fact, there are no "routines" or strict training here. Because dance comes from within—it's a natural part of you. You don't even need to think about it. Believe it or not, *your body is begging to move.*

It doesn't need a manual. It needs *permission.*

Wiggle your shoulders. Shake your head. Slowly rotate your arms in a circle. Close your eyes and sway. Let the movements come naturally, and listen to what your body is telling you.

More than anything, be mindless.

Shelve the mental chatter, the critic, and the internal judge, and focus on your body and what feels good.

Don't think; just *move.*

In the 25 years I've spent as a movement therapist, life coach, and workshop and retreat leader, I have created an amalgamation of different techniques to formulate the ChakraMental Method™, an approach that is carefully designed to help you feel better, express more, and genuinely connect with your heart and soul. This method is partially based on the Kripalu DansKinetics training, now called Kripalu YogaDance®, that I learned from my former teacher, Dan Leven, in 1997.[2] My training was a mixture of teachings from the Kripalu Center for Yoga and Health, the School for Body-Mind Centering, and the grandmother of movement therapy, Anna Halprin, who redefined dance as a tool for healing. Now, the ChakraMental Method™ combines each of these learnings, and an uncountable number of others, to help further my mission: to make the world a better place as humans learn to love themselves and learn to lovingly respond, interact, and communicate with those around them.

The freedom of expressive movement is a wonderful approach to healing and empowerment, emphasizing the natural joy of movement rather than technique or form. Through both guided and free-flowing creative movement, you'll connect with your inner voice and guidance system. This is not a traditional dance class with choreography and memorized routines. The music, especially, is where it gets fun and creative. It is hand-crafted to be a movement journey with tunes from around the world and rhythms ranging from stillness to pulsing tribal.

On top of being fun, this movement method can also be an engaging workout, guiding your movements using the intrinsic qualities of the elements (fire, air, wood, water, metal, earth, and ether) and connecting you to each energy center of the seven-chakra system. By using these seven "ChakraMents," a combined approach to chakras and elements, you will be able to access and tap into feelings and energy centers within you that you may not have even imagined. My clients and groups have been exuberant with feedback that experiencing and practicing this method has released old thoughts and traumas that navigated their lives from the shadows. They have experienced more freedom from pain and increased mobility, and through building their confidence, they have fallen in love with their bodies, souls, and *lives*! Once you gain that connection with yourself, it's amazing how you can connect with others. But it all starts with you and your body.

I'm going to say this again: *Bodies don't lie. They don't know how to lie.* But believe me, they can feel and tell you things your heart and mind do not want to hear. You may call this feeling your intuition, an annoying nagging, or a gut feeling, but whatever you call it, there's one thing you need to do—trust it. You cannot always rely on your mind, which has been influenced by your family, culture, or other people's beliefs, to help you out in every situation. Many times, your body and mind disagree on which immediate action to take in response to a trigger. The body sends signals based on pleasure, pain, and survival, but the brain eclipses these bodily messages with the "culturally appropriate" reaction, ultimately leaving you vulnerable. For example, you may not leave a room full of people even though your stomach twists in knots from anxiety or your head pounds with a headache from overstimulation—all because your brain says running out of the room wouldn't be the "socially acceptable" thing to do. In this scenario, ignoring your body and listening to your brain could lead to an emotional bomb going off, either externally (lashing out at someone) or internally (berating yourself for not having a "normal" reaction). In moments like these, you need the skills to trust and listen to your body.

I'm speaking from experience here. By listening to my body and acting upon its message, I uncovered a painful deception in a horrifying and violent event. What I suspected, but couldn't fathom, was really happening to me. Here's the story.

When I got pregnant with my second child, my relationship with my husband changed. I couldn't really discern why it happened, but it did. He was an artist and would spend most of his time in his studio across the street from our downtown condo. I was running our restaurant and catering business, so I saw him drinking more than ever, entertaining every woman who glanced his way. I also suspected he was using drugs with some of the restaurant staff.

I was three and a half months pregnant, and a part of me thought our life could return to normal. That was my brain talking, wishing, and convincing me to "put my head in the sand." My gut, on the other hand, was in a constant state of unease and anxiety, especially when he started staying overnight in his studio following nights of partying. While my brain tried to think its way back to normalcy, my gut, my inner wisdom, knew things wouldn't be getting any better. Guess which one I finally listened to?

One night, when my husband still hadn't returned home after 2 a.m., I felt an intensely visceral clenching in my stomach. At this time of night, I knew all the bars were closed, so I climbed out the window of our condo and paced the flat roof, looking for him like a woman on her "widow's walk," waiting for her sailor to come home from the sea. All of a sudden, my body couldn't take it anymore. Nothing was changing and something was wrong, and I had to go find out for myself. I picked up the baby monitor so I could listen in on my first child who was asleep, grabbed the keys to the studio, and marched outside. I opened the door to the studio and was immediately hit in the face with blaring music. I walked up the concrete steps, all my nerves on edge. And what a sight I walked into.

My husband was dancing with a young woman—both of them naked and drunk out of their minds. *Well, there it is, my body! Here's what you had been warning me about all along!* Seeing that confirmation of my intuition was overwhelming. And as for my husband and his dance partner, they didn't notice me even though I was screaming his name. Finally, the girl saw me and started shouting and pointing. My husband turned toward me, his face erupting into an ugly expression of utter disbelief, and started yelling, "What are you doing here? Get out!" He began to advance toward me angrily, but my body saved me again. I instinctively reached out, picked up a wine glass, and threw it on the floor. I hoped that the shattered glass would stop him from coming toward me barefoot. But somehow, he made it across and physically pushed me—his wife carrying his three-month-old child in her belly—down the concrete stairs, all the while cursing and yelling, "You don't belong here!"

Struck by the most intense fear, I ran back to the condo, grabbed my firstborn, and went straight to my mother-in-law's guesthouse in the country. I called her and told her everything that happened, and she, along with my sister-in-law, came over to look after me. I reached out to one of the women in my group therapy, who helped me shift my focus to my unborn child and reminded me that he was experiencing this same trauma through me. Per her advice, I sat in a warm bath trying to calm the nerves of both me and my baby. I spent more than an hour whispering to my child, telling him that he was safe. And telling myself that I was safe. My body had told the truth, and after confirming its untainted wisdom, I began to build a strong relationship with my body and its messages.

It took several years for me to "exorcize" the trauma of that night. By taking a difficult look inside myself, I was able to see the psycho-genetic patterns and misogynistic beliefs that had been navigating my life from the shadows. I recognized that this awareness was the first step to healing, and through diligent work, I slowly released these traumas and regained control over my emotions and actions.

I believe that using the body's messaging system is a definitive way to point life decisions in the way of confidence and joy, away from cycles of trauma, hurtful beliefs, and emotional suppression. I hope you, the reader of this book, will soon understand and adopt this sentiment too. My wish is that by relating to my stories and those shared by my clients, you will try out the concepts and exercises in these pages, release anything holding you back, and embrace the unknown power and confidence within your heart and soul. You'll crack the code of body language. You'll learn how to be curious instead of critical. And most important of all—you will, by the end, become the navigator of your own life. Just as I did, decades ago.

Your body is like a dependent child. If you neglect it, it will die. This book is the process by which you can nurture, heal, and listen to that child. I'll share everything, from funny to deeply intimate anecdotes of my life, in the hopes of breaking any barriers to love and enjoyment. Each chapter details one of the seven elements and its accompanying chakra, as well as hand-picked exercises, music, and videos, so you can take it step-by-step, using different forms of media to guide you. Don't worry about getting it right. After all, the core idea is simply to listen to your body, so any move is the "right" move. You can learn at your own pace. I'll be right by your side, guiding you through my heart and with my passion for the power of these tools. The best feeling is knowing you are not stuck and can learn and change your ways. After all, that's the beauty of human brains; neuroplasticity makes it possible for you to change. Hear that again. *It is possible for you to change.*

Every word, sentence, and technique within these pages has been curated by me. This means that you also get to curate your own experience. For anything you read, take away what feels right for you, and let go of the rest.

Welcome to the beginning of your journey with the ChakraMental Method™. Slow down. Get fully in your body. Feel what's there. Embrace it, no matter how dark and painful. Connect to your wild heart.

Your body is talking all the time. *Are you listening?*

CHAPTER ONE
BODIES DON'T LIE

No one can be stagnant for long. Your body replicates new cells every day. Within seven years, all the cells in your body are completely replaced, making you an entirely "new person." Your blood moves constantly. Your heart beats on. Your lungs breathe. In and out. In and out. All of it without you even making an effort. So, you can't be stagnant even if you try—your body moves, and so do your thoughts. The best you can do is be *intentional* about it.

No one is ever too young or old to act with intention, to change their lives, to begin feeling the way they want to feel.

When I, pregnant with our second child, walked in on my husband dancing naked with another woman, my world shattered, along with all the dreams and visions I had of my future. Never had I been exposed to or experienced anything this horrifying in my life and instantly felt paralyzed in the face of my fear. What now? I had no idea, but I *did* know that staying curled up in a catatonic state would not move the acid coursing through my veins out of my body and mind, so I left for Wyoming. *This trip will put space between me and the situation while I figure out my next step*, I hoped.

Some people may stop here and ask, "Wouldn't isolating yourself on a trip just trap you in your own head? Wouldn't you get lost in an endless loop of the same thoughts, over and over?"

Sure, that was a possibility. But I was in so much pain and confusion. I was feeling alone, suffocating in a mental cesspool, and my body knew the only thing that could free me was taking action. Any kind of movement was better than lifelessly steeping in my own nasty mental stew!

My 10-day trip to Wyoming was the best decision I could have made. Putting space between me, my husband, and the environmental triggers gave me the opportunity to *observe* and *respond* instead of being subjective and reactive. (We will revisit this concept again, so take note.) And since I had a travel schedule, I kept busy and had a routine. There was no time to even *think* about being stagnant. Driving endlessly on those long Montana roads was a great distraction, opening me up to many spontaneous, new experiences. The beautiful, rich land called to something buried deep inside me. My body bubbled with energy and childlike wonder, and every minute, I excitedly asked myself, "Wow, what's around this corner? Could it be a new beginning?"

I didn't know it then, but I was already taking my first step toward healing. I was *moving*. The first step to connecting with yourself is to take the plunge, break out of the lethargy that's keeping you shackled in one place, and force your body to move and express. I had all this energy within me—most of it negative, born out of the terrible trauma I had just faced. But by deciding to go on that trip and taking that big, gigantic, crazy first step, I turned all that energy into something positive and worthwhile. I was getting to know myself.

Feeling and guiding all that energy—positive and negative—stored within our body unlocks a wave of transformative power. A power that helps you ride the waves of life. Our bodies hold our stories and traumas and will reveal these truths through movements, which release us from limiting and debilitating thoughts. Somatic movement works through this concept by supporting physical mobility, mental stability, and neuroplasticity. In other words, it nurtures your mind and body to become one. Whole. Complete. It helps you start asking those same questions I began asking in Wyoming: In what areas does my life feel stuck? In what areas are my ideals being blown to bits?

And the scariest question of all: *Who am I now?*

You'll find, just as I did, that the moment you start asking who you are, you will start morphing into the person you're supposed to be. Even if you want to fight it. What's that old saying? "People plan; God laughs."

Are you ready to take your own first wild step? We're jumping with both feet into some life-changing territory here.

EMOTION IN MOTION

When people think of movement, they think linearly: sports, gyms, running marathons. It's not enough to just play a sport either. To be a "good" athlete, you need to move in a certain way and train your body and neural pathways to respond in a narrowly consistent manner. There is not much creativity in hitting a tennis ball in the back corner of a tennis court, only a reliance on an invariable, basic swing. The skill only builds when you learn how to hit the ball in the perfect place on the racquet every time.

Most humans find comfort in knowing what is expected of them and what comes next in the moments ahead. Some adamantly defend their repetitious worlds, their "comfort zones," and steer away from anything new and unknown. Unfortunately, life is never predictable, and those who stay rigid crumble at every unexpected event. There is a definite need to have some flexibility, adaptability, and "go with the flow." You need to be able to embrace your many different approaches to life and use these as tools, not curses. You need the balance of both rigidness (for the commitment and dedication to complete a task) and flexibility (to dodge a curveball but still reach a goal).

This is where intentional movement can shift your perception, reaction, and approach to any obstacles by allowing you to simultaneously stay disciplined *and* adaptable, all while taking the mental and making it physical.

When I say "movement," I'm talking about way more than simply moving your *body*; it also includes moving your mind, your emotions, and your soul. This brings up the old "chicken or the egg" debate. Which comes first: the *thought* for change or the physical *action* toward change? One thing I know is that necessity is the mother of most change. You need a nudge, a reason to shift. This nudge shows up as chronic physical pain, mental pain or negative self-talk, and/or emotional pain (sadness, anger, or fear). I believe that bringing awareness to this pain in the body and physically changing its habitual direction is an extremely powerful and workable modality for anyone experiencing discomfort.

In psychotherapy, the concept of bringing consciousness to your ways of thinking and communication is known as a paradigm shift.[1] By thinking about subconscious thoughts and feelings with a specific vocabulary, you can make them more tangible and, therefore, easier to manipulate.

The alternative (refusing to think or talk about the needs of your body) will only escalate any oppressed trauma. Ignoring your body does not negate its desires; your emotional state will come forth one way or another, maybe in the form of a clenched fist, copious sweating, a racing heart, chronic pain, or breathing difficulty. While outward symptoms may only occur when you're experiencing or thinking about a traumatic incident at first, soon you will find yourself responding inappropriately to all sorts of situations—stressful or otherwise.[2] With as much medical evidence that exists to discourage the bottling of emotions, many solutions are available as well: therapy, yoga, meditation, and somatic movement.

Your mind is a powerful entity and runs your life, whether you like it or not. Your thoughts, feelings, and perceptions have been forming since you were a child, perhaps even before then. Usually, your cultural environment supports those beliefs to the point of reflexive thinking, coming to conclusions without consideration for anything else. So, this entity can keep you in a thought loop that brings you pain. This is where I say, *get out of your mind and into your body.* Movement gives your brain the opportunity to shut down or shut up. It allows your body to lead and move you through to the other side of your pain.

You'll find that you're not only *externally* engaged but also *internally* engaged; you're able to feel and express those emotions hidden within you. You find the strength to free yourself, open up, and *talk* to your body instead of feeling disconnected.

Think about how you feel working out in a public gym versus in a private space, such as your home. When you walk into a gym, you likely focus on the external body, wanting to lose weight or build muscles. Then, you see yourself in the mirror . . . and all you see is your body. When surrounded by other people who are all concerned about "getting in shape," you may only pay attention to your outward appearance. Yes, you may have experienced all of the psychological and physiological benefits of working out, but how connected do you feel to your inner self? To your body's needs? To your real feelings?

Now, consider somatic expressive movement through dance. In my studio, there are no mirrors. The purpose? To keep your attention internal and not externally triggered. Some of the most important senses I create for you are safety, security, and confidentiality. This is an oath every student and I take so that you feel comfortable and supported to go past your defense mechanisms into the depths of your shadow and reveal to yourself the hidden fear—the root of anger, pain, anxiety, or any other negative emotion you may be feeling.[3]

The music begins, and I ask you to gently close your eyes—though not completely; we don't want you losing total situational awareness and accidentally kicking or bumping into someone. Once you have what I call your "soft eyes," you can move in whatever way your body leads, responding to your inner, subconscious drive. Your mind is now back in your body, listening carefully, moving in a way that feels natural, and experiencing every muscle as it stretches and tightens. Your physical internal body is brought to your awareness; your emotional body is expressing itself without any boundaries. You are connecting, completely and wholly, to how *you feel*—not how you think others see you. That's the power of somatic expressive movement. The more you're able to move your mind, body, and emotions, the more empowered you will begin to feel.

By definition, somatic movement therapy is a process that awakens awareness of the body. As the word "soma" means "the body as perceived from within," somatic movement is any movement—yoga, dance, grounding exercises, breathwork—that intentionally focuses on the internal experience instead of the end result.[4] In the somatic world, the physical is an expression of the psychological. Through movement, you build the skills to slow down and listen to your body, express what's been oppressed, and rather than fight, freeze, or take flight, you learn one, all-important way to tackle every situation: *flow*.

Michael Lott's Story:
From Engineering to Healing

Angel and I had both recently left corporate America. From there, our similarities only continued to mirror each other: we were both from Knoxville, Tennessee, had moved away and moved back at the same time, and wanted to find something bigger and more impactful than what we had been doing professionally. It seemed like we were living our lives in parallel—we even started our own holistic practices at the same time!

My fondness for Angel knows no bounds. She is one of the most creative and spontaneous people I know. She's a firecracker who lives loud, almost like a female James Bond with the way she races cars and jumps out of planes. I remember this one time when we were driving around in her little Mini Cooper convertible with the top down, blaring loud music, singing at the top of our lungs, hair flying everywhere, and being so incredibly present in that fun, life-defining moment. Every second I spend hanging out with Angel is like that—fun and life-defining.

Back when I left the corporate world, I wanted some of that spontaneity to rub off on me. I was an engineer, and while I loved my work, I wanted something more meaningful. As a noise and vibration specialist, my approach to engineering was both intuitive and analytical, but what was most interesting is that I found the way we talk about vibrations in the field is very similar to how it's spoken of in the holistic world. I had grown up in a metaphysical, energetic, and spiritual family, so I had always been drawn to that form of healing as well. Before I knew it, my heart was telling me this was what I needed to do. I had to take everything I knew about vibrations and apply it to help myself and people through healing work.

Besides, corporate America was sapping my energy to the point of detriment. Every day, my body would shout, "You are done with this!" I tried to power through, but my body did not like being ignored. Plus, I didn't even have the language to describe how my body was feeling, not to others or to myself.

One day, I had to leave work early because my back hurt so bad that I could barely crawl into my house. I surrendered to the floor as my body told me, "Give in. Everything is being taken care of. Just surrender and relax."

I started to listen. The part of me that I had been pushing aside for a while wanted me to move back to Tennessee, to let go of the corporate world, and to embrace spirituality. Learning to trust my heart and body was a huge learning curve for me, but I devoted myself to it. I decided that I would do what my heart was telling me, like Angel always did. I took a page out of her book—I leaped.

I earned a certificate in mediumship and performed energetic reading for 10 years while also leading several workshops and teaching others how to do it. And while I started with this type of intuitive arts and counseling, I was looking to become more grounded in my body, and so I turned to Angel, who introduced me to the expressive arts—specifically dance and movement. There was an inner dancer in me that longed to come out and express himself. When I saw Angel express so fully through her body, it was inspiring and unbelievable. She was so in tune with her body that when she danced, it looked like the most effortless, creative, freeing activity in the world. I wanted that.

I had been spiraling in my life, but I wanted to express that through creative and expressive arts. So, I made the natural choice: I signed up for one of Angel's classes. She taught me how to relate to and attune to my chakras and the elements—and how they translate into beautiful movements. Her teachings also helped me build a deep trust and understanding in the language of my body, which I use every day in my work as a counselor/therapist. I learned everything from using the earth element to ground myself, to immersing in the ether element to tune into the universe around me. Angel changed my life through her classes. Even now, I frequently use the language of the ChakraMents to make sense of my emotions, actions, and reactions to the point where it's automatic. Once the ChakraMents enter your life, they change your internal thinking forever—I know they changed mine, and every day, I am thankful that Angel taught me how to express myself.

Now, I may not be perfect since trusting my heart over fears or societal distractions can sometimes take intentional effort, but as I follow my inner truth and the right spiritual paths, I am, every day, becoming one with my body and mind.

DANCE YOURSELF FREE

Before I tell you more about the science behind the ChakraMental Method™, let me share the story of how I got here, how a somewhat lost single mother of two kids became a somatic movement therapist and confidence coach. It's a wild ride, so strap in.

I was back in my city after the Wyoming trip, and while I was still married to my husband (we were trying to work things out), I no longer lived with him. He stayed downtown, and I lived on a 10-acre farm with my two boys. I was running this big household and being a mother, and it was . . . *exhausting*. I'm sure all the women reading this book who have devoted their lives to other people know what I'm talking about. My one solace during that time was my massage therapist who kept me grounded. He was a true healer. He knew all about my husband and my family, the trauma I had undergone, and the struggles I was going through.

One day, he handed me a magazine and said, "Check this out."

It was a thick magazine that listed about 220 workshops hosted by the Omega Institute of New York. I took one glance and scoffed.

"Who has the time for this?" I asked.

In my mind, all I could think of were the responsibilities I was tasked with. I had other people to look after! Things to get done! And besides, it's impossible to find time to do *anything*, let alone work on my life . . . right?

A few days later, I flopped onto my bed and leafed through the magazine. A teacher's training popped off the page at me: "We were born to dance! Danskinetics is a dynamic dance practice intended to enliven your body, mind, and spirit. Rediscover your instinct to move and dance with soul and passion." *Yes!* Everything inside me agreed like this was the light at the end of the tunnel. Dance: how much I loved it yet left it behind. It sounded like freedom and exactly what I needed to move to the next level in my life. Most of all, something inside me wanted to work on myself, despite knowing the sacrifice it'd require.

The somatic movement certification was a 30-day class located on the remote campus of the Omega Institute near Rhinebeck, New York, nestled in the Berkshires. The program started in 10 days—how was I going to pull this off? My "gut feeling" turned into a hell-bent pursuit. I made the hardest decision ever: I entrusted my husband to take care of our two toddlers for 30 days. Before I knew it, I was packed and on a plane headed to Albany, New York, and after a mountainous cab ride, I found myself in the most peaceful place I had ever experienced. I didn't know anyone . . . or really what I had signed up for.

I was separated from the rest of the world, from the everyday, from the dull anxiety of encountering my husband, and from the stress of making sure my boys had what they needed for their mental, physical, and emotional growth. And while my thoughts threatened to turn to fear— fear for my boys, fear of my husband's negligence, fear of something bad happening and not finding out about it—I calmed myself down. I was determined. I was going to heal. I was going to get back into my body. There was at least one far-away phone booth to keep me connected with my boys, my world. It had to do for the next 30 days.

During that month, my entire life changed. I connected so deeply with movement, with myself, and with my body that I could feel myself becoming lighter. I could feel the trauma and the negative energy leaving through every pore in my skin. This was it.

Dance. Dance. Dance.

Feel. Feel. Feel.

Every day, we moved for at least six to eight hours. And when we weren't dancing, I was learning about body fluids and the connection of the body systems with the emotional, mental, and physical brains. I now had my beautiful, spiritual soul in the driver's seat, understanding the significance of subtle, connected movements that made all the difference. I studied all the connections to the body, interpreting its language—the vocabulary of "body speak"—and opening to my own ancient somatic intuition.

Sometimes, it takes a group doing the same activity to draw you out of your mind. A group effort pulls you out of the "individual alone" and into collective collaboration. One drop of acid alone can burn a hole in steel. But dilute that acid in water, and watch it become neutral and benign. My time at the Omega Institute allowed me to experience life on a bigger scale, bigger than my marital troubles and responsibilities.

When the time came, I was sad to leave the all-encompassing support from my teacher and classmates, but I was excited about the unknown possibilities that lay ahead. I had learned how to love myself, *all of me*, so deeply that I actually saw the world and my situation with rose-colored glasses. Having secured my certification, I knew this was my path to pursue, no matter what. I wanted to dedicate myself to helping people heal the way I healed. I wanted to help them move past all the traumas and hurtful experiences. It's possible even if it feels impossible. I know that feeling well, after all. And I made it through.

LET'S GET SCIENCE-Y

After my first brush with somatic movement therapy, I went on to study and earn various other certifications. In the years that followed, I created two group classes and maintained a large client list for individual sessions.

For more than two decades, I've helped clients and led my own programs. Over these many experiences of continuous learning and teaching, I've distilled everything into one methodology: the ChakraMental Method™. The differentiating factor is that the ChakraMental Method™ embraces mindful, cognizant, and sentient movements influenced by music and rhythms that correspond to the seven elements in nature and draw from the ancient, energy medicine of the chakra system. I created this method to specifically help people release the traumas and stuck energy that cause physical, emotional, and mental pain every day—and to create the freedom to do what moves them by using the *ChakraMents*.

The ChakraMents combine two principles: seven *elements* and their associated *chakras*. Each chakra helps you tap into a specific area to release and channel the energy stored within. According to Hinduism, the chakras correspond to the seven energy centers in the human body: root, sacral, navel, heart, throat, third eye, and crown chakras. It is with a deep understanding of these chakras that the ancient forms of yoga and Ayurvedic medicine were developed, and it also forms the basis of the ChakraMental Method™. These chakras centers can influence your health and well-being, and subsequently, you can improve yourself by intentionally working on your connection with these energy centers.[5] And while the *chakras* allow you to put language around what your body is experiencing by giving you the parameters to ask relevant questions regarding your discomforts, the associated *elements* tell you how to remedy negative feelings. In other words, the chakras and their location in your body give you the scope of questions to ask yourself, to recognize an issue, new or chronic, and to start a conversation with your body to find answers.

We will dive into each ChakraMent in the following chapters, but here's a quick overview, along with the physical and emotional qualities they strengthen.

ChakraMent	Movement Qualities	Physical Abilities	Emotional Qualities	Result
EARTH 1st Chakra: Root	Give in to gravity, rebound, swing, sink down to Mother Earth	Define your **bottom line**. Build **support** within yourself. Gather energy to **rebound**.	Develop trust. Surrender freely. Practice resilience.	Self-trust
WATER 2nd Chakra: Below the belly button	Flowy, syrupy, sensual	**Flow** with grace. Find the **path of least resistance**. Embrace your **sensuality**.	Nurture emotional flexibility. Learn to be adaptable. Connect freely.	Self-pleasure
WOOD 3rd Chakra: Solar plexus	Arrhythmic, chaotic, shake it out	Lean on your **bones**. Thrive in **structured chaos**. **Jiggle, giggle, and shake** off bad energy.	Clear your mind of unnecessary obstructions. Make way for new growth. Self-nurture.	Self-support

FIRE 4th Chakra: Heart	Pumping, rhythmic, moving to the beat	Get your **heart pounding**. Let the **rhythm move you**.	Tap into your desires. Fuel your passion. Release anger. Be unstoppable.	Self-love
AIR 5th Chakra: Throat	Verbal and physical expression, using breath to inspire and move	**Express** yourself. Use your **voice**. Enjoy your **breath**.	Use movement, words, and sounds to release your emotions. Release what is oppressed. Feel relief.	Self-respect
METAL 6th Chakra: Third eye	Straight, deliberate, intentional	Refine your **goals**. **Direct** yourself toward your needs undistracted.	Strengthen commitment. Find your dedication. Fine-tune your focus.	Self-discipline
ETHER 7th Chakra: Crown	Cloud-like, angelic, all-encompassing, moving meditation, gentleness	Bring awareness to the **lightness** of your body. Float **cloud-like**. Allow all emotions and thoughts to **exist at once**.	Integrate the mind, body, and spirit. Connect to your highest self. Radical self-acceptance.	Integration

These ChakraMents help you accomplish four objectives crucial to your well-being:

1. **Shift** from the status quo to where you want to go.

2. **Acknowledge** the pain, discomfort, stuckness, and stagnancy.

3. **Express** emotions verbally and through movement.

4. **Connect** to inner wisdom, creativity, self-love, and other people.

By moving in a specific elemental way, awareness of what is stuck or missing in our lives becomes apparent. For example, the pain connected to trauma can be touched, brought out from the shadows, and released through consciously connected movements as opposed to letting avoidance or fear of the trauma dictate your every action. Unearthing your trauma is freeing. Some call this getting in touch with your shadow. It empowers you to become stronger and more confident, especially in controlling your life and claiming your rights. It lets you move past the obstacles and pursue your goals with the lightness of a bird, no longer bogged down by heavy emotions.

Understanding the science weaved into our muscles and tissues and the psychology of body and mind responses is integral to getting the full benefit of the ChakraMental Method™. Before we explore the seven ChakraMents and various related exercises, let's understand five important physiological concepts: body cueing, body mapping, body speak, neuroplasticity, and stimulus and response.

Body Cueing

To understand body cueing, let's do a quick exercise.

Part one: Close your eyes, and imagine yourself moving your leg straight up in the air.

Done? Good.

Part two: Read the passage below, and as you read it, imagine yourself performing the actions too. (And if you're not reading this sitting in a park or on a bus, then maybe you can get up and actually do it!)

Take a deep breath in and exhale. Do it again. And this time, notice your ribs expanding with each breath. As you pay attention to your ribs, slowly straighten your spine and your head. Now, tighten your leg into a straight line, feeling your knee lock into place. Carefully feel the muscles in your leg. They will be taut and brimming with energy. Keep that tightness as you take another deep breath, pulling apart your ribs, pushing your shoulders back, and lifting your leg up in front of you in a straight line, pointing your toes forward. Feel that stretch from your toes to the base of your thighs. Slowly bring your leg down, exhaling and relaxing your ribs and shoulders.

Notice a difference between the first exercise and the second? I bet you do. So much is going on in the second scenario. You're still performing the same action—lifting a leg—but your whole body is activated and intent on performing this action. Doesn't that feel incredible? Did you notice sensations in your body that you never noticed before?

This is body cueing. By describing every movement and sensation in your body, I'm cueing all your muscles and your mind to pay attention while you perform an action. You're not just doing something; you're doing something consciously with 100 percent focus. In most of the exercises in the book (and in the videos you'll be able to access throughout), you will engage with body cueing every step of the way. This will completely change the way you interact with your body, helping you connect with yourself more than ever.

Body cueing bypasses your mind and lets your body do the talking.

In essence: ask the mind to do something, and notice how it says, "I never learned how."

Ask the body to do something, and see how it responds, "I can do this."

Body Mapping

Body mapping is the identification of different areas (or chakras) of your body, what they represent, and how they can be affected. The locations in your body where any discomfort, pain, and sensation show up give you a clue to the issue or trauma that you've buried. Body mapping provides you with questions to ask at the moment, brings the trauma to your awareness, and gives the body a common language to communicate. This bypasses the brain and its acculturation, justification, guilt, and shame that stuffed the trauma in your tissues in the first place.

THE BODY'S SEVEN MAIN CHAKRAS

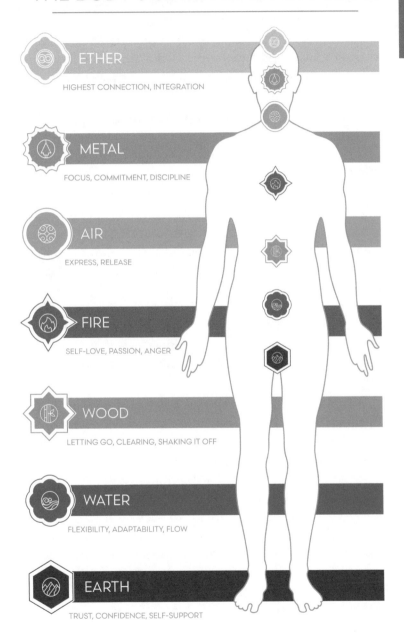

ETHER
HIGHEST CONNECTION, INTEGRATION

METAL
FOCUS, COMMITMENT, DISCIPLINE

AIR
EXPRESS, RELEASE

FIRE
SELF-LOVE, PASSION, ANGER

WOOD
LETTING GO, CLEARING, SHAKING IT OFF

WATER
FLEXIBILITY, ADAPTABILITY, FLOW

EARTH
TRUST, CONFIDENCE, SELF-SUPPORT

The "ChakraMental Human" diagram is a roadmap to understanding your own body and its messages to you. As you go through each chapter, you'll accumulate knowledge about each chakra and its elemental correlation, develop an understanding of your internal dialogue, and learn how to shift it when needed for spiritual growth and happiness. What is inside you directs everything outside of you.

The chakra gives clues to the why, and the element is the remedy.

Body Speak

Your body has its own language to describe what it's feeling and sensing. And as with any new language, the process of mastering it—both speaking and understanding (and I mean really understanding, accepting, and appreciating) it—can be just as difficult as taking up Spanish, Mandarin, or Swahili. However, practicing this language and implementing it into your life is one of the most important triumphs you can accomplish. These are the navigators, the captain of your ship. If you are looking for self-awareness or direction, the concept of body speak is an essential starting point.

Just as every word in a language has a meaning, every sensation in your body has a meaning too. For example, the sensations in the back area of your body could indicate a chronically unremedied wound from your past. Sensations in the front of your body are the manifestation of current experiences. The sensations on the left are your feminine side, representing your ability to receive and embrace. Conversely, your right half is the masculine side, which deals with the masculine energy inside and outside your body and how you present yourself in the world. Legs are how you move yourself through the world, feet and ankles are your foundation, and knees are your support. Spinal issues up into your neck have to do with flexibility in your life. Shoulders are how you take on responsibilities and tasks, and the throat is how you express the collaboration between your heart and head. And finally, eyes are how you see the world—your perspective.

The best example I have of body speak involves one of my own experiences. As I had experienced trauma while pregnant with my son, he developed chalazions (similar to styes) on his right eye. The chalazions became so chronic that his doctor scheduled him for surgery.

At that time, I was seeing a healer who was trained in the holistic arts. She helped me interpret what my son's eye was saying. Apparently, his body remembered the pain I'd gone through with his father and felt the trauma I experienced, and his right eye (masculine) was screaming the internal pain that he felt and saw. The healer suggested a remedy of putting a warm compress on his eye while both his father and I (united) held him as he squirmed. My son would try to wiggle out of our hold and start crying in an attempt to avoid the emotional pain, and he would fall into a deep wailing until he was done. We knew he was finished for the session when he relaxed in our arms again. His father and I did this daily, and in 10 days, his eye was cleared of the chalazions and I canceled the surgery. He viscerally felt our focus on his healing and the collaborative support we gave him to acknowledge what was stuck. He was able to cry out the trauma, fully releasing it and healing.

Neuroplasticity

The most common definition of neuroplasticity is "the ability of the brain to change in response to experience." *Newsweek* science writer Sharon Begley's book, *Train Your Mind, Change Your Brain*, reveals that the brain is capable of altering its structure and function and even of generating new neurons, a power we retain well into old age. The brain can adapt, heal, renew itself after trauma, compensate for disabilities, rewire itself to overcome dyslexia, and even break cycles of OCD and depression.[6]

Think about your drive to your best friend's house. Do you need directions? I imagine your answer is: not now. But the very first time you drove over, you had to rely on your trusty GPS. So, what changed? The simple answer is that you learned the way. The complex answer is that your brain picked up on certain triggers each time you took that route—a bus stop, a McDonald's, a giant tree—and these triggers add up to the collection of directions stored in your brain. Now, every time you look at that tree, you react; you associate it with the road to your best friend's house. In other words, your brain learned a route through association, and now you don't really have to be conscious about how to get there. It has become reflexive, and you drive to it without thinking. The cool thing is the brain is not stagnant or a fixed organ; *it can change*. This specific ability of the nervous system and the brain to change its response or activity by reorganizing its neural connections is called neuroplasticity.

Your brain is flexible enough to learn a new way of action and reaction.

When you experience trauma, your brain shifts and develops new connections associated with that bad experience. So, now, whenever your trauma's trigger is provoked, your body immediately associates it with your past experience and sounds the alarm, bringing on your fight-or-flight response. If you've ever felt scared, stressed, or anxious seemingly out of nowhere, thinking something like, *I messed up. I'm not good enough. I feel unsafe*, then this is likely the cause. But not all hope is lost; just as your brain changes to accommodate this new trigger, so can it change to release your trauma.

Neuroplasticity allows you to heal. By engaging with the ChakraMental Method™, where guided exercises will help you acknowledge, feel, and safely express your traumas and emotions, you will be able to harness the ability of neuroplasticity to let go and find freedom. As I said, your brain is capable of change; the ChakraMental Method™ gives you the power and the tools for change.

Choice, Stimulus, and Response

Connected to the concept of neuroplasticity is the idea of putting *choice* between *stimulus* and *response*. Choice is a powerful opportunity. It allows you to choose between how you're *programmed* to respond and how you *want* to respond. For example, if you're someone who has experienced severe body issues, a giant bowl of cookies in front of you (the stimulus) may push you to eat the entire thing even if they make you feel sick (the response).

But stop right there. Let's bring choice into the equation.

You see that giant bowl of cookies, you become aware of your urge to stuff your face with them, but you take a moment to give yourself a choice: *Either I can eat them all and feel very sick, or I can eat one and walk away.* Simple, right?

Putting choice between your stimulus and response sounds easy, but it's not. It takes awareness and demands focus, requiring you to clear your mind so you can build better habits. The "why" of why you want to change is where you must train your brain to focus.

This is the reason ChakraMents are foundational; they nourish all the skills and qualities you need to acknowledge, connect, feel, and express. For example, **air** brings awareness, **metal** strengthens focus, and **wood** clears your mind. But first, you always need to start with grounding—yourself, your mind, your body, your soul. Take root so you may grow.

The **earth** element awaits.

Journal Exercise

Grab your journal. Settle in and take a big breath. Write down all the things you like about yourself. And be generous. For example, you could write, "I am a good listener for my friends," then list all of your top skills, and then everything that makes you happy.

Another ritual is to write down any negative, corrosive thoughts about yourself, then crumple up and burn the paper with those thoughts. Watch the fire consume all that negativity and bless the smoke as it carries them away. Writing down these thoughts brings the unconscious to your consciousness. And with the awareness of all these thoughts—good and bad—you can intentionally heal and better yourself, physically and mentally.

CHAPTER TWO
TRUST EARTH

EARTH **1st Chakra:** Root	Give in to gravity, rebound, swing, sink down to Mother Earth	Define your **bottom line**. Build **support** within yourself. Gather energy to **rebound**.	Develop trust. Surrender freely. Practice resilience.	Self-trust

As I drove down the long roads of Wyoming, making my way from Old Faithful to Yellowstone, I passed through a small town called Driggs. Population: 280 people. At a crossroads, I saw a beaten-up, handwritten sign, and I slowed down enough to read it: "GLIDER PLANE RIDES. 2 MILES."

The whole point of being on this trip, of putting space between me and the situation back home, was to explore and find myself. I've always tried different things: I've been called an adrenaline junkie, and for some reason, I've trusted left turns to nowhere. To live truly is to break patterns and avoid ruts! What's a better way to get a different perspective, a view of the whole picture rather than just one moment, than being high in the sky in a tin can with wings? I knew that the only way to carve out a new version of myself was to step into the unknown. I made up my mind: "*I'm doing this!*"

I followed the signs down a dirt road to an airstrip next to a big barn. The woman directed me down the road to a diner where the pilot was having lunch.

My heart began to pound with excitement (and for once, the cause was not anxiety).

I stepped through the door of the diner, a small, 50s-looking greasy spoon complete with linoleum flooring and side stools rimmed with metal. All five people in the diner turned their heads toward me, and I walked forward, confident, with determination in my eyes. I asked the guy behind the counter about the glider plane pilot, and he pointed to a man sitting on a stool at the far end, wearing a checkered shirt and denim overalls.

"That's Jerry," he said and then turned away to go about his business.

I walked up to Jerry and asked him about the glider planes. Could I go up in one?

He looked at me closely and then nodded. "Alright, let me finish my burger."

Jerry made short work of his food, and before I knew it, I was following him out of the diner and toward a barn at the back.

I paid him for the ride—it wasn't much—and one of the other guys in the barn hooked a cable to a single-propeller plane that would pull us. Jerry gestured toward the glider, and I quickly got in.

We're playing fast and loose with the word "glider" here. It looked more like one of those toy planes you might see in a store: just a long, metal shell with two big wings, and that's about it. Jerry got in the seat in front of me, the propeller engaged, and all of a sudden, I felt a jerk. We were off! I held my breath in total awe of what was happening. How long had it been since I felt so completely unrestricted? A long, long time, that's for sure.

Once we were high enough, the cable dropped and we were solo, gliding up and down on the air currents. It was incredibly quiet and peaceful up there, even though there was not much more than wing flaps and a rudder to guide us. Jerry didn't chat, so it was just me, my thoughts, and a burgeoning sense of freedom. I was so immersed in this experience, the panoramic aerial views of snow-capped mountains, the calming sound of the wind whooshing by, and the serenity of being totally absorbed in the moment, that my body hummed with positive energy, grateful that I was finally listening to it.

Before that moment, tuning out the external chatter and trusting the small voice inside had been rare and difficult. But sitting in that metal flying cocoon, that's all I had.

Trust in the pilot I just met.

Trust in the journey that was unfolding in front of me.

Trust in the universe that I am safe.

And trust in myself and the decisions ahead.

Being so high up, all my problems seemed so small. When we landed and I exited the plane, I felt renewed, as if I had been through a spiritual carwash and somehow gained the fortitude to face whatever was up ahead. I had to become ungrounded to find this peaceful confidence and then land back on earth to establish a new sense through my body, to take root in the omni-supportive Mother Earth. Mother Earth, the epitome of love and unconditional support, encouraged me to reach higher into the unknown, creating the next step of my evolution. The rebound. I knew I could do it all—make changes, start anew, grow, be strong, take control.

I felt rooted in my reality like never before.

THE STARTING POINT

Earth is the bottom line. It bestows unconditional love and support, earning the name *Mother Earth*. Mother Earth encourages you to reach higher, go for your dreams, and step into the unknown with the assurance that you have safety. You know that you may fall, but you will never fail. Earth energy breeds faith and trust in you *by you*.

The earth element urges your roots to grow (through a mother's encouragement) but also helps you stay grounded (by listening to a mother's wise words of caution).

As discussed in chapter one, the ChakraMental Method™ is integrated with the ancient Vedic chakras of Ayurvedic science, and the earth element is connected to the root chakra, called *Muladhara* in Sanskrit, situated at the base of your spine. The spine supports, allows you to stand straighter and with purpose, and has your back (literally), just like the earth element. All healing starts there.

Earth: Questions to Ask Yourself

- Do I feel grounded?
- Do I encourage and support myself?
- Am I supported by my family, community, and friends?

When you're disconnected from the earth element—and, by extension, disconnected from yourself—your body will scream out some telltale warnings, trying to release the emotions and discomfort in any way possible. Often, this kind of release is painful, disruptive, and negative. Acknowledging these symptoms is critical, yet most people suppress them. If you don't know what your body is telling you, how can you help it heal?

To know where you want to go, you need to know where you *are*. We start with the root chakra and earth because it is your foundation of radical self-acceptance. You need to look in the mirror and honestly ask yourself, "Who am I now?" By grounding yourself, you can create the space to look inside. To dive deep. To figure out who you are by listening to your body as it resonates with the earth. And once you understand your bottom line, you can forgive yourself and others and trust yourself to grow past it all.

Ask yourself: What would you do if you knew you couldn't fail?

Earth Movement Exercise

To understand how connection with the earth feels, let's do a quick grounding exercise that will help you embrace three important aspects—the earth element, the root chakra, and yourself.

Sit comfortably on the ground with your legs crossed. Close your eyes. Feel your sitz bones sink into the earth, and begin to relax the body. Ask your joints to release any pain and become aware of your spine. Notice how your head is balanced on your neck, and let your thoughts spill down your spine through your tailbone and into the earth.

Let your tailbone root in the dark earth, and imagine it holding you upright, supporting the entire weight of your body. Now, you are rooted deep in the soil like the roots of a tree, so you can never waver, never shake. But you can sit still in peace, trusting the earth to hold you in place. It anchors your body and your mind, fostering deep confidence and peace.

Give in. Surrender your anxieties, worries, and burdens. Send them down deep into the ground through your spine. The earth will absorb your burdens, just as a mother would. Rely on your courage, fearlessness, and self-assurance to help you bounce back. Rebound as high as you can, knowing that even if you fall, you will never fail because the earth, your ultimate safety net, will receive you.

ONE WITH ME

Earth's strength, a hard-as-a-rock pillar, allows you to trust, release, forgive, and grow. Everyone falls, especially when chasing after goals and visions, so you need earth to regroup and bounce back. In your life, where else do you find this kind of empowerment? Think back to your roots—your family, your tribe, and your community.

As much as I hope your support system loves you unconditionally, many people feel like they're more commonly being buried in toxicity rather than uplifted. From a community lens, social anxiety is at an all-time high, with 15 million Americans experiencing social anxiety and, of them, 75 percent having symptoms as early as childhood.[1] In public, socially anxious people don't trust themselves enough to go against the status quo, even when it'd be beneficial to what they want and what their bodies are telling them. Instead, they give in to external pressures from those around them.

"Sure, I'll have another drink even though I don't want to."

"Sure, I'll go on a date with you even though I don't feel safe."

"Sure, I'll babysit your toddlers even though I'm drained of energy."

Why do we do this? What is the internal dialog, the driving force? Probably this:

"If I don't comply, then there's something wrong with me."

"I will be rejected."

"I'm different from them."

Self-sacrifice is a sign of self-distrust. Actually, I'll take it one step further. Ignoring and disrespecting what your "self" wants is a red flag of self-*neglect*. You may not know what is mentally best for you, but your body knows and will usually give you a sign if you ask. Ever heard of muscle testing? It's an alternative method by which you can assess the physiological and psychological state of your body by applying gentle pressure.[2] Just by touching and feeling your body, you can hear it speak.

Listen to your body—do you feel uncomfortable around certain people? Take action to distance yourself from them. It can be hard to know who is unconditionally loving you and who is leeching off of your love, but your body knows. Call it an uneasy feeling, an intuition, or whatever you want, but if you don't act upon it, you will suffer the consequences. Trust me, I know.

Before my marriage exploded in my husband's studio, we had problems. Surprise, surprise. I experienced stress around the complex roles of "sexy" wife and mother. Every day, I felt so unlike myself. My body was uncomfortable, but I pushed it all down and tried to "perform" like I thought I was supposed to. But the real me could never turn into Betty Homemaker overnight. My body suffered as a result: a fistula developed at the base of my spine, right at the center of the root chakra. It was painful to even sit.

Every time my stress levels peaked, the fistula became angry and inflamed. My immediate family and most of my good friends (my support system) were not close in proximity, and the lack of support from my husband just made it worse. My body was in so much discomfort and pain that it needed a release, so the movement classes I taught became a saving grace. I was able to park all my worries and anger outside the studio and enter a surrendered place of service to my participants. This experience grew as a gift I gave my clients later—to be completely present with others who are looking for help, assistance, and release for themselves. I became so immersed in the present moment that when I left the studio, the worries and anxieties were gone from the door where I had parked them.

My group classes, which I held religiously two days a week for years, became my tribe, and we worked through challenges and delights together. In a safe and sacred place, we could break down the emotional barriers and break free into life's joy together. Using conscious movement and syncopated music, we were able to shift, acknowledge, express, and heal with the support of each other. Here, I learned the profound power of group movement and therapy. The different, unique perspectives and the various kinds of support are exponential in one's healing. They were my grounding, they were my Mother Earth, and as their empowerment grew through the use of the movement principles, I too was healed.

The fistula, after being there for seven long years, had to be surgically removed. I had let it fester for too long, and despite ultimately finding solace in movement, it was too little too late.

But once I began to live my truth as someone who loves to be in her body, enjoys expression, and helps others heal, I stopped suffering. I expressed myself as a holistic healer, using somatic movement and its principles to empower class participants, clients, and audiences to connect with themselves and each other in a loving way.

I cannot emphasize enough how important connecting with yourself is. You can't connect with other people if you don't already have the structure for self-support. This is another reason why we start with the earth element: it helps you ground yourself and develop self-reliance, so when the time comes, you can uplift someone else.

Symptoms of Disconnect with Earth

- Fatigue and sluggishness
- Constipation or diarrhea
- Uneasiness in your body
- Feeling anxious, insecure, unstable, and shaky
- Experiencing chronic depression

ON SOLID GROUND

One of my childhood friends grew up in a household of rejection. Her parents didn't want her from the second she entered the world, which was made obvious by the way they treated her even as a baby, putting their needs ahead of hers, neglecting her, and even oppressing her as she grew up.

One evening, while I tutored her in math, her mom yelled from the kitchen, "Why are we even trying? You'll never be good at math!"

I'm not sure what came over me, but I stood up, walked up to her mom, and said, "Don't say that to her! I'm here to help, and she's trying. *You're* not helping!"

Flash forward several years later: my friend was working for a prestigious, well-established law firm … that had some secrets. The issues between the paralegals and lawyers were nefarious, which became apparent to my friend when she took a business trip to assist one of the lawyers.

On that trip, one of her coworkers tried to come on to her. Offended, she stood her ground, and told him, "No." She had been suspicious and knew with every fiber of her being that this would be wrong, despite the extravagant pleadings from him. She fended him off more than once, and finally, he backed off. But the worst was not over.

When they returned from the business trip, she found herself demoted to the basement where she was only tasked with archiving and filing. The reason was clear.

Instead of taking it lying down (literally) like her predecessors, she stood up for herself and eventually for them. She filed a class-action lawsuit against one of the largest, oldest law firms in the state. And fought it alone.

Despite her admirable actions, she experienced pushback, not from her acquaintances or coworkers but from her *family.* Her family, the people who had undermined her since the day she was born, offered her no support. She held strong, and after much turmoil and many nasty tactics to stop her, she won. I consider her one of the strongest people I know.

She is a perfect example of the power of cultivating the earth element within. Self-reliance, self-support, self-respect—all of these are born and raised from the earth element. When her family did not support her, she had to form another tribe for that companionship and loyalty. Soon, women who were wronged by the law firm in a similar way came out of the woodwork and stood with her. The trust in herself helped other women trust themselves. She was building a community without even realizing it.

If my friend had relied on her toxic family for permission and encouragement, where would she be today? Probably in the basement of the law firm, head buried deep in a filing cabinet. But she found a way to believe in herself, to tap into her root chakra, to draw the strength from within. She strengthened her foundation, straightened her shoulders, and bounced back.

Earth Affirmations

- I trust myself.
- I listen to my body and its messages.
- My unique way to rebound builds confidence and self-respect.
- Mother Earth will always be there for me. Whenever I need to collect myself, I connect to her soil.

"DANCE LIKE NOBODY'S WATCHING"

Do you remember those bumper stickers that read "Dance Like Nobody's Watching"? It's possible the somewhat-cliché phrase doesn't hold much meaning for you at first glance, but after sitting with the words and really thinking about them, how do you feel? When was the last time you danced, with or without another person present, and felt completely free and uninhibited by what others might think? For some, the answer is "never."

Years ago, I had a new client schedule an individual session with me. Despite all the reassurance and guidance I gave her, she simply could not move. Not *wouldn't*, but *couldn't*. Her body refused—plain and simple. Obviously, that's not healthy. Bodies are designed to move. They need it. The fact that her body was so rigid and fearful made it clear that something was going on underneath the surface. Her body was telling the story of what happened to her.

The very first thing we did was connect with the earth element as she was in desperate need of some grounding and unconditional support. It was when we moved to the second chakra, with syrupy, sensual music to move her hips to, that she started to cry.

I grabbed one of my dancing scarves, placed it over her head and shoulders, and said, "Dance like nobody's watching."

As she began to move, her body released what was stuck in there for so long. She shared the trauma that had been holding her back for her entire life. When she was about 15, one of her teachers groomed her and became her "lover." Despite knowing about this, her family did nothing. That's some deep-rooted familial distrust there. Not to mention, being groomed from such a young age created a disconnect between her feelings (which screamed that something was wrong) and her body (which experienced nubile pleasure). No wonder she was paralyzed! She had no self-trust, no support system, and no awareness of her beauty and creativity, which had been blocked.

Movement allows you to separate from your mind and your community and to connect with your body and your truth. Within that space, you can observe your challenge and feel and judge what is right for you. Solutions that once seemed unattainable will feel completely doable. Why? Because you're grounded in your body, in reality.

You have control over your decisions. You have trust in yourself and thus the universe.

Movement grants you the power to maneuver away from discomfort and listen to the story behind the pain. Let Mother Earth absorb all your anxieties and fears. Tell her your stories. She gives you a solid ground to stand on and will nourish your roots with the very energy of life.

Move like you're one with the earth. Because you are.

Align with Earth

Here are some resources to help you align the earth element within you and beyond you.

Earth Spotify Playlist:

Move with Me Videos:

Bonus: Grounding Meditation

This earth exercise can be done at your personal pace and needs. It's particularly great to do as a start-of-the-day meditation or as a way to get grounded and clear the head in any situation.

Stand on the ground, preferably barefoot in the earth, but this can be done just fine with shoes on concrete.

Close your eyes slightly or all the way. Feel your feet: your heels, the sides, and the padding in front. Wiggle your toes, and drum them on the floor.

From between your big toe and second toe, grow a root down through the floor into the earth below.

Keep growing your roots, past the rocks and shale, and deep into the center of the earth into the molten, fiery, energetic center. Let your roots become straws to suck up this energy, and draw it back up into your feet. Feel it energize all the bones and muscles in your feet, those things that support you as you move.

Draw this energy up the ankles, and feel this give lift to your joints there. Now, move it up your shins and calves into your knees, and again, feel the space it brings to your knee joints. Continue moving it up to your thighs, the large muscles that move your body from one location to the next. Feel your thighs burn with energy as it passes into your hip joints, lubricating this area to roll and release when you walk.

Allow this energy to migrate into your lower belly, the dantian, where nurturing your sensuality happens. This is your creative center, so notice how it ignites. Feel the energy wash over your stomach and soothe any discomfort there. As it rises into your chest, let it kindle your heart, your passion, and your desires.

Take a deep breath into your lungs, and pull this lovely energy up and over your shoulders. Let it fall down your arms like water and stream off your shoulders like a waterfall, taking with it all the "should"s and the weight of your worries. As the energy moves to the throat, let it clear any blocks to you speaking your heart. Clear your throat. As this energy makes it up through your face, let it melt any tension in your jaw or forehead. And when it reaches the top, open your crown chakra, and let it out to connect with the divine.

There. Now you have connected heaven and earth. Your body is the conduit for both.

FLOW INTO WATER

WATER 2nd Chakra: Below the belly button	Flowy, syrupy, sensual	**Flow** with grace. Find the **path of least resistance**. Embrace your **sensuality**.	Nurture emotional flexibility. Learn to be adaptable. Connect freely.	Self-pleasure

Instead of wallowing in negativity and fear, I always try to look for the "lesson" and seek spiritual adventure. That's why, at times of overwhelming and aching stress, I sometimes find myself on the back of a horse.

I've always felt a special connection to these animals, having ridden both Western and English horses since I was five years old. They have been a source of true escape for me, especially when I feel restricted and caged. The wind whipping through my hair and nature unfolding in front of me as a wild creature allows me to sit on its back, experience unfettered freedom, and solely focus on the moment before me—there's nothing like it. Especially,

especially because, since birth, everyone has tried to shape and mold me into "perfection," society's little "angel." That's just it though. There's nothing *perfect* about *wild*.

At a time when I hoped to embrace the childlike spirit within myself and maybe find some answers to bigger questions, I booked a spot at a horse therapy retreat. The field had eight rescued Mustangs in it, and we were allowed to walk amongst them to feel and see their reactions to us individually. All but one let me pet it and stand with it—*a kindred spirit*, I thought, being a wild one myself.

The Mustang's name was Thera, a horse with genetics of the first wild Mustangs in the US. Before being rescued by the farm, she'd been abused, meant to reproduce foals before eventually being shipped off to the glue factory. Because of her past, she didn't like humans; she'd been stripped of her original purpose on Earth. Of course, I didn't know this yet as I walked up to her. When I reached out to stroke her neck, she jerked away from me and then looked intensely into my eyes. I felt her very clear boundaries, like she was saying, "That's close enough." When we reassembled, Thera's caregiver said she was amazed at how close I was able to get and that no one except her caregiver had been able to stand within six feet of her. I learned a much-needed lesson about my own boundaries and trust that day.

The next afternoon, I sat on the dirt of Thera's corral and, with my eyes closed, began to connect to her. I braced myself by placing my hands firmly on the ground beside my crossed legs. Thera circled me so closely that I could feel her hooves landing right beside my fingers.

I began to cry as my heart burst open in full connection with her. A shared vision expanded before me: we exploded into a field, running and running—wild and free.

She looked at me and said, "Come on, Wild Heart! This is who you are—Wild Heart!"

Tears ran down my cheeks. In this beautiful moment, she was channeling the message: "Do not rein it in. Do not harness it. Do not hide!" Tears, tears, tears of understanding.

She gave me answers that validated who I am. She proved that surrender and vulnerability are the most powerful paths to the heart. Since then, I decided that no matter what I do, I need to do it through and with my wild heart. I need to channel it, surrender to its messages, and flow over any boulders that block my path. And along the way, I am grateful to help others steer and steady their boats on their own journeys.

And so, WildHeart Expressive was born. Through my company, I help others find and follow their joys, connect with their inner selves, channel the elements within them, and set sail on their exciting, wonderful voyages.

The ChakraMental Method™ starts with earth—feeling grounded and supported while letting any struggles sink deep into the soil as Mother Earth nourishes you. Then, as I felt riding on the back of Thera, you flow like water, learning how to be flexible, adaptable, and unstoppable, like how a river flows over and around debris and fallen trees to move in one direction: *forward*.

WATER CONNECTS ALL

Close your eyes, and picture a running stream, deep in the mountains. How does it flow? Does it stop because it encounters a rock? No, it finds a way to keep moving. It may hit a large boulder and crash in waves and small droplets next to it or around it, but no matter how it decides to carve a path, you can be assured that it's always moving forward.

Sometimes, adaptability will be the only thing that keeps you going in life. Having the fluidity of water is all about being able to shift and change with the tides of life—emotionally and physically. If you want to move forward, you better be ready for a whole lot of change. It is easier on you in the long run to bend and not break. Knowing what to shift is where our bodies' messages can help. Pivoting includes changing routines, unhealthy habits, perspectives, and mindsets. Whether it's moving *away* from these things that hold you back or moving *toward* the things that edify you, it begins here with the water element.

Water picks a path of least resistance. It is not about confrontation but rather about finding a course through the many challenges of life. Trying to fight every problem stalls you and takes up more time and energy that you won't get back. Time that can be better spent elsewhere. When you encounter a point of contention—a failing relationship, a dead-end career, or even a physical challenge like scaling a mountain—flow with it, take the path of least resistance, and be flexible enough to surrender to it and let it lead you.

Water: Questions to Ask Yourself

- Do I need *more* water in my life?
  - Am I inflexible?
  - Am I rigid, non-negotiable, or uncoachable?
  - Where am I stuck or blocked? Have I hit an impasse?
  - Do I have fears about money or the lack of money?
  - Do I feel sensual and sexy in my body?
  - Am I comfortable connecting with others?
- Do I have *too much* water in my life?
  - Am I wishy-washy?
  - Do I have no direction?
  - Do I lack the motivation to move forward in my life?

The water element is associated with the second chakra, found below the belly button in the creative center of your body. This is where passionate, fire energy is tempered into creation. It's where babies are given life. The Sanskrit word for the second chakra, *Swadhisthana*, translates to "where your being is established." With so much inventive and prolific power literally channeling through the birthplace of the self, the second chakra challenges your imagination and dares you to find innovative, out-of-the-box solutions to all the problems that hold you hostage. The water element says you will discover a way past your obstacles, but only if you let go of the things you cannot control (i.e., external situations and other people) and allow yourself to break *free* of the dams in your life. Bust through them like a flash flood, and flow like water to a new level.

Soft, swirling, and sensual, water invokes the innate ability for flexibility, sexuality, and creativity. Relating to the feminine principle of nurturing and community-building, it connects you to your inner self and then to others in an all-inclusive way. Flowy and adaptable, hydrating and nourishing, it also draws opportunities to you, such as relationships and money, like a whirlpool with you at the center. Conversely, water also helps you release destructive, blocking emotions, more often than not in the form of tears escaping your eyes and flushing out pent-up sadness.

Think of it this way: not only is 60 percent of the average human body made of water, but the brain alone is 95 percent water. Put in obvious terms, having a water deficit isn't good. People without enough of the water element often feel stuck and rigid, like their whole lives fit in tiny, constricting boxes. Nothing spontaneous or unexpected happens without water; every day seems as boring and cookie-cutter as the last. The whole future feels gray, pale, and stagnant—in other words, completely and utterly dehydrated.

In the same way that having *too little* water can be draining and bland, there can be times when surrendering *too much* to the water element can cause serious harm. Think about what happens to water when it sits out for too long: it becomes rancid. The remedy is bringing in other elements like fire and metal—everything in moderation and balance.

To have the water element present is to be all-encompassing. It goes all around you, cradling you and making you feel comfortable. Notice how the second chakra is located near your belly button and lower belly. Now think: Where was your first connection to another being? In your mother's womb, through the umbilical cord. You were surrounded by fluid and the necessities of survival. Therefore, the water element deals with connection; it is how you connect to other people intimately through physical communication and sexuality.

Those who have mastered the water element and second chakra make the people around them feel accepted, comfortable, and included. They're those open-minded, optimistic people who feel warm and inviting, like you could never do wrong in their eyes because they respect and accept you just the way you are. One of the most endearing qualities of these folks is the ability to meet conflict with *curiosity*.

A word of caution here though: because these in-tune water aficionados are so loving and accepting of all, there's the risk of allowing other people to walk all over them like doormats. Have you ever had a friend or family member who constantly seems to bow down to the needs of others? Have you ever told someone to put themselves first and do what *they* want, not what *someone else* wants? When people constantly give in to others, they have an over-connection with the water element. In other words, they are too subservient and have let go of too much control over their own lives. Too much of anything is not good for you—the same logic applies to the elements too.

Think about this in terms of sexuality. Some people— much of the time, women—feel uncomfortable setting boundaries with their partners. But if they fail to communicate what they want and don't want, then their boundaries keep getting pushed, and they develop traumas around their own sensuality and interpersonal relationships. Sure, to make relationships work, you need to go with the flow at times, but there are also times when you must take a stand and voice your needs. The balance of giving and standing your ground is subjective, but here's a little clue to look for: when going with the flow and "taking one for the team" starts to feel like you are depleted, disrespected, and receiving nothing in return, then it may be time to reassess "why" you are giving and "what" is your desired outcome. Failing to do that will just cause more misery on the road ahead and bring up challenges that you simply cannot adapt to. Forming self-depleting habits in one aspect of your life will flow into other parts of your life.

A balance needs to be achieved. Yes, flow freely, but you don't have to go with the flow *every* time. Boundaries are important; know when to gush forth and when to move slowly, taking the time you need to carve your own course.

> ## Symptoms of Disconnect with Water
>
> - Uterine cysts
> - Chronic bladder issues
> - Kidney stones
> - Painful sex and lack of sensuality
> - Lower back pain
> - Feeling "stuck"
> - Indecisiveness
> - Feeling overwhelmed, anxious, and stressed

PATH OF LEAST RESISTANCE

Challenges are a given. Life is riddled with adversity that you have to overcome to continue on. The things that stop most people, however, are not the challenges themselves but rather their reactions to them. When something gets in your way, ask yourself: What is my resistance? Do I fight it, run from it, or become paralyzed by it? Why can't I flow when I'm overcome with the fear of something new, something out of routine, out of the ordinary, or out of schedule?

More often than not, you'll find that your flow is blocked because you're not allowing change. Change can be scary. You can't prepare for the challenges of life; if you could, they wouldn't really be challenges, would they? But you *can* prepare your mindset. You can ready yourself to respond to the unknown with flexibility. With the intention to flow, embrace it and let the experience take you somewhere new. Put your oars in the canoe, lay back, and let the current take you. Maybe the change that comes out of it is exactly what you need.

I understand that what I'm asking you to do is not easy. It takes hard work to focus on strengthening the water element within you. Personally, the element that comes most naturally to me is the water element, but even I've had days where it just seems so hard to go with the flow.

I remember, during one of "those" times of the month, Aunt Flow, the bane of every woman's existence, came to town. On top of what had become the everyday stress of my life—running an environmental non-profit organization, preparing a teenage boy for college, and being available 24/7 for my 91-year-old mother—I was also PMSing. It's a tough time for me and for everyone around me when I go through this every month. I was at the end of my very short rope that day, with every little thing annoying me to no end. I was uncomfortable, in pain, and my mind was buried deep in a fog. I had given up. *Throw the whole day away*, I thought. *Let's try again tomorrow.*

That's when someone came along, prodding me to shift my perspective: my beau presented the idea of us going on a motorcycle ride.

For a second, I felt a little irritated. *Can't I just stay at home and wallow in my sorry state?* But when I looked out the window, the beautiful sky, sunshine, and perfect weather all beckoned. They seemed to say, "You're facing a challenge? Just flow with it."

Even getting ready for the ride frustrated me though. Fumbling around, I must have dropped everything I picked up at least once, my anger rising with each item clanking to the ground. (This is something I call the "dropsies." It's just another headache that happens during this time of the month for me.) After much annoyance, I finally made it outside, where I plugged my ears with headphones and blasted music by Styx, one of the many 80s bands I love and had recently reconnected with. As head-banging tunes blared in my ears, I put on my helmet, hiked one leg over Black Beauty (my Harley Davidson Sportster), and shot off down the road.

In Greek mythology, the River Styx separates the earth and the underworld. Apropos, since I felt trapped somewhere between this plane of existence and the next. I began to sing at the top of my lungs, letting the music wash over and through me, feeling like a river, roaring and flowing fast, fast, fast. The speed of the bike, the loud music, and the intense release of my emotions, rushing out of me in tall, cathartic waves, all matched the internal intensity of my PMS symptoms. Soon, I was neutralized and felt like I was back to my normal, calm self. That ride was Rx for PMS.

Clearly, I had neglected the water element for too long—no wonder it manifested as physical symptoms. The uterus is connected with the second chakra, after all, and allowing my emotions to flow instead of stopping in my tracks, I was able to reconnect and replenish. In the beginning, no part of me wanted to go on that bike ride. It was difficult for me to pull myself together and do *something*. But when I did, I let the bike ride take me on a new, transcendental journey, and through this, I was able to shift my perspective and emerge transformed.

PMS is one of those challenges that no one has any control over. And circumstantial obstacles, ones that you can't control, are what the water element is best at navigating. In the earth element, you would simply let this challenge drop to the ground and sink deep, letting the earth absorb the fallout. Great for acknowledging why you're hurting and trusting yourself to get through it, but water is better for moving past the pain and changing your mindset. You simply flow *around* it. The challenge can remain where it is—you just need to take the path of least resistance and move on, leaving it behind.

The one thing you do have control over, however, is your perspective. All the emotions you feel are a result of your life experiences. While growing up, if you fell down, how did your parents react? If they made it easy for you to get up and keep playing without freaking out, chances are that facing challenges is a lot easier for you. But let's say, when you fell, you heard words like, "You're so clumsy." You might internalize this and assume that you *are* clumsy and helpless. Two similar situations but completely different experiences, resulting in a totally different view of yourself and your abilities. Your perspective influences everything, but the good news is: *it can be changed.*

Sometimes, your perspective influences your beliefs and can become rigid and inflexible, leading to isolation and judgment. I had a friend in college who was terrified of auditioning for the school dance troupe. Her terror was a result of her experiences as a child: one day, while dancing freely through her house (as little girls tend to do), her aunt laughed at her and said, "You look ridiculous. You will never become a dancer."

My friend was devastated. However, she still loved to dance . . . just no longer in front of other people.

In college, she still held on to that belief. She may have loved to twirl and move in private, but there was no way she could ever become a real dancer. Despite that, I still encouraged her to audition. As it turned out, she was quite good, even without regular, formal training. So good that the dance troupe accepted her. She busted through the internal voice in her head (the voice of her aunt) and was so thrilled when she got to perform for the next four years for our school and the public.

Sometimes, certain feelings are deeply ingrained within you and your tissues, as in the case of my friend. But most of the time, the negative voice inside is *not* yours. When a negative or knee-jerk thought occurs, ask it, "Whose voice are you?" You might discover that the disruptive voice belongs to a parent or some other adult whom you looked up to. Gravitate toward encouragement and leave the naysayers in the dust, including the ones inside your own head.

Diane Smith's Story: Movement Is Celebration

Ten years ago, I was hit by a drunk driver. My condition was severe, but despite my injuries, I lived—thanks to an orthopedic surgeon and physical therapy. However, my body was extremely limited. I tried to work on myself, but I encountered roadblocks. First, my legs were so weak that even when I tried building bone density, I found that my upper half overcompensated in every workout. This meant that I couldn't push myself up off the floor without using my hands, and doing a squat was out of my league. Second, the culture around fitness was intimidating. When you haven't always been athletic or "the perfect size," some trainers can be condescending—and even downright rude. So, when my friends did not agree to join me at a movement class, I almost gave up. Yet, somehow, I found the resolve to take care of my body.

No, I decided. *I need to do this. I need to make a commitment to myself and my body. And I need someone by my side.*

This is when I met Angela—or my "Angel."

Angel has the gift of meeting people where they are. When I signed up for my first somatic movement class, the most I could do was march in place, but I never once felt uncomfortable, judged, or intimidated. Everything about Angel said, "You are loved and welcomed here," something that was new and unfamiliar to my previous experiences in the world of fitness and movement. I kept going back to her classes, and each day, I could feel myself stretching and dancing to the point where I wasn't only moving but also having *fun*.

When my first nephew had gotten married years before, I was still in a lot of pain due to the accident. My body was so out of shape that all I could do was stand on the sidelines and watch everyone dance. In my heart, a deep wish bloomed: *I want to dance with everyone too.* A few months after taking Angel's classes, the day of my second nephew's wedding arrived—and I had never looked forward to anything else more. I was first on the dance floor and the last to leave it! I mean, I dropped it *low* in front of my whole family, and they couldn't believe their eyes!

Somatic movement gave me the power to *celebrate* life.

I believe our bodies are designed to heal. If you're willing to show up and put in the effort, your body, mind, and spirit will follow. As of 2024, I'm 64 and I never thought I would ever be pain-free or able to dance the way I danced at that wedding. I was so present on the dance floor, so in tune with my own body, that not once did I worry about who was watching.

All this confidence and self-love is a result of my leap of faith. Just try out the different exercises in the book— at least once—and see how you connect with them. I guarantee that you'll want to try again and again. But first, take those baby steps. Test out the waters. Pick an element and try those movements for yourself. And, most importantly, remember to have fun with it!

A shift in perspective can often help, which is what happened when I saw the truth about my friend's self-doubt and pushed her to break out of her comfort zone. The tricky part is finding that shift in perspective for yourself. What's even harder is making sure the new perspective is helpful, not more harmful than what you started with.

Here is an example of the differences in perspective. In an art class, 20 students sit in a circle and sketch the same apple placed in the center. However, if you were to look at each of the drawings, you'd see completely different works of art; the same apple would be drawn from 20 different perspectives. Now, think of your challenges and the way you currently perceive them.

- What words do you use to describe your problem?

- What words do you use to describe yourself? What about the words you use for others?

- How different could your view be if you shifted two seats over and looked at your problems from a different perspective?

- Does this perspective let you move on, or does it stop your flow?

- How can you change this perspective?

Though I encourage you to try this out, note that certain trauma responses can be harder to face, redirect, and change. But by approaching traumatic issues through the body's response mechanisms, you can make it less scary and put space between you and the trigger so that you can develop the perspective to effectively change it. Though, I would suggest this only be done in a safe environment with a trained therapist. The goal is to achieve your own inner peace about your challenge. Not always easy, I admit, but this is how you know you have truly moved on and that this experience or person does not trigger you anymore.

Water Affirmations

- I am adaptable.
- I am creative in my flexibility.
- I have the ability to flow and self-soothe.
- I embrace all of me—the good, bad, beautiful, and challenging—with grace.
- I am gentle with myself.

FEAR RESPONSE

Most of our intense, harmful feelings can be reduced down to a fear of "something." Fear of loss, fear of change, fear of pain, hurt, guilt.

Fear is the biggest blockage in the stream of life.

I'm not saying fear is a bad thing. It's a natural reaction to immediate danger that keeps you safe, like when you're faced with an aggressive animal or person. Back in the Stone Age, fear helped humans avoid predators like saber-toothed tigers and dangerous situations like wildfires and thunderstorms. It assisted humans with preservation back then and continues to do the same now.

But let's be real: most of your fears today don't involve "survival of the fittest" or life-or-death scenarios, even if the preservationist part of your brain thinks so.

In the modern world, people are more afraid of emotional consequences like not being good enough, rejection, abandonment, or heartbreak. So, when fear happens from the thought of an undesirable future (your spouse leaving you, losing your job, never achieving your dreams, being seen as "worthless" or "unwanted"), then your motivation is to take "flight" and avoid the problem, to "fight" the uncontrollable, or to "freeze" and become emotionally paralyzed.

Here's a quick example to simplify these learned responses. It's probable that somewhere in your life, you "fell in love" but the other person did not reciprocate this love and dumped you. The preservationist (the primal, emotional, and survival) side of you likely created a new rule to live by: "I will never let that happen again. The pain was unbearable, and no one will have access to my heart."

To this, I ask: Do you want to create your future from your past fears, or do you want to create your future from your desires?

I have another example for you, this time one that hits close to home.

I was a daddy's girl. Every evening, my dad would return home from the hospital where he worked as a surgeon. I'd jump in his lap and tell him all about my day, and he'd normally listen to me and give me a lollipop he brought back from work, picked out just for me.

But one night, something distressing or unsettling must have happened at the hospital because, when my dad walked through the door, his demeanor just screamed,

"Leave me alone." I fell into our routine: I wanted to tell him all about my day. But he waved me off and didn't even have a lollipop for me.

Since that moment as a child, the rejection triggered a survival response that gave me a hard and fast rule to live by: men whom I love and respect do not listen to me, and therefore, I need to become louder, smarter, and sexier to get their attention . . . and to survive emotionally.

When I entered the corporate world as a 20-something, I was outspoken, super competitive, and sexually confident. My motto? "No grass grows on a rolling stone." Meaning, I never stuck around in relationships to work things out or make things better. Nope, I just moved on, never looking back. Now that is a fear response that uses the water movement in an unbalanced way.

Broken down, FEAR can stand for "False Expectations Appearing Real." Notice how the word "expectations" refers to a *possibility* in the future, not a *reality*. Not many people have the gift of fortune-telling. It's likely you can't see into the future and don't know what will happen, no matter what that anxious "what if" part of your mind tries to tell you. You make up your fear. And getting past an imagined reality is as simple as remembering the typical primal responses: fight, flight, or freeze.

Well, I add one more to the list: *flow.*

It's okay to acknowledge your fears. Don't fight them. Don't walk away from them. Allow them to be there. You need to stop and sink down into the water element. This can be a sad and emotional moment that needs to be felt fully.

Then, *express* your fears. Give them a voice. Listen to what is said. Maybe if I had a mature flow response to my father, I would have just allowed him to have his feelings and not been affected by them, knowing that our relationship would probably return to the way it had been the next day.

Here's a little perspective hack. When in an intense emotional state of fear (or any of fear's secondary manifestations, such as anger, jealousy, anxiety, or sadness), use the Splash Model. Try to see the moment as a drop in a bucket full of emotional water—water that has been collected from your life's experiences. When you can pull yourself out of the intense moment or feeling, you will give yourself space to look at the trigger (the incident or words that evoked the fear response). Taking an emotional step back gives you the ability to shift your perspective and change your reaction. This concept is the one that empowers you to come out of devastation, depression, and distrust and dissolves the triggers, changing your reactions to thoughtful responses and allowing you to move on. *This is the power of the water element.*

"THE SPLASH MODEL"
HOW TO EXPLAIN THE PROCESS & FEELINGS
DURING TRANSFORMATION

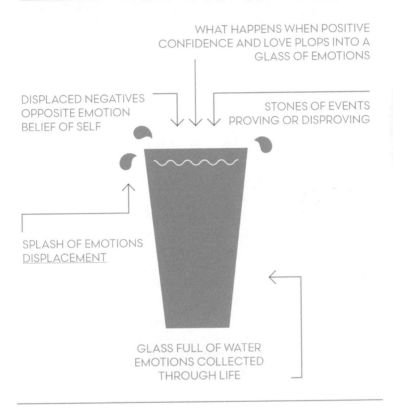

WHAT HAPPENS WHEN POSITIVE
CONFIDENCE AND LOVE PLOPS INTO A
GLASS OF EMOTIONS

DISPLACED NEGATIVES
OPPOSITE EMOTION
BELIEF OF SELF

STONES OF EVENTS
PROVING OR DISPROVING

SPLASH OF EMOTIONS
DISPLACEMENT

GLASS FULL OF WATER
EMOTIONS COLLECTED
THROUGH LIFE

WHEN "GOOD" DISPLACES "BAD"

PHYSICAL: WHEN YOU EAT GOOD AND BAD FOODS, THERE'S ONE
ENTRANCE. AS THE FOOD IS DIGESTED, THERE'S ONE EXIT. THE BODY
NATURALLY KEEPS THE GOOD AND REJECTS THE WASTE.

MENTAL / EMOTIONAL: WHEN GOOD ENTERS, THE BAD SPLASHES
OUT. CHOOSE THE GOOD, TRY TO KEEP IT, AND REJECT THE WASTE.

Water Movement Exercise

Water is a connected flow. From trickle to stream to river to ocean, it will find a way.

Put on some music that is flowy, sexy, sensual, feminine, and syrupy. Imagine diving into a vat of honey. Suspended, swimming, feel your body as one organism, not just a bunch of parts put together.

Start by swaying your hips. Then, include your thighs, moving them in a circular motion and connecting the bones in a watery movement as with a mermaid's tail. Bring this sensual movement into the mid-belly and your ribs, moving your spine like a snake. Soften your shoulders and shrug off the "should"s, letting them melt and roll down your arms like water. Move your arms like big paintbrushes, painting the world around you. Then, bring all this flexibility up into the neck, rolling your head and feeling any stiffness or pain. Think about what is upsetting you—keep moving, swaying, circling, engulfing this feeling in your movement. Ask what it is and what it needs. Dislodge it and let it flow with your movements. Whatever you do, don't stop—keep flowing through the intensity of your emotions. This could be expressed as tears or anger, or maybe you just need to wrap your arms around yourself in a hug.

Keep moving. Let your body tell the story of what you are feeling. I have observed in most clients that underneath anger is sadness, and once the anger is expressed, sometimes the real root of sadness shows up. Keep moving even when you want to stop.

Move with your feelings.

Let them be there.

Let them be okay.

You are okay.

Now that you are aware of the triggers, have deeply felt the feelings, expressed them through movement, and let out the waterworks, how can you see the situation differently? Is there a different response? Time to let your creativity out and come up with a different perspective and reaction. It is time for self-nurturing. You can put the music back on and dance in the new response; let your body feel the difference. Now that it is in your body, you can put it into action.

Fear is the dam that constricts and blocks life. Once you touch it and acknowledge it, it can put cracks in the concrete and leak out, resuming its natural course and relieving built-up pressure. You'll feel for yourself how it rises to the surface like a bubble, pops, and disappears. What lies underneath often is intense grief for something lost—the way you wished someone had reacted, the relationship you wished you had with someone, the opportunities you wished you were granted.

An age-old question lies at the center of most fears: What will other people think?

This is at the root of it all. *What will other people think?* This disables people. It minimizes their dreams. It stops them from doing the things *they* love. The water element embraces creativity and nourishes your dreams, hopes, and wishes. It embraces you. And what does this fear do? It produces a creative block and amplifies the inner saboteur, saying nasty things like, "Everyone's going to think you're crazy" or "No one is going to like what you create" or "You aren't good enough."

The water element exemplifies the femininity present in everyone—men and women. While these qualities may be suppressed in us, bringing them forth through our fluid movements and uninhibited emotions can help us get in touch with our bodies and minds and experience loving ourselves more. Learning how to be gentle, understanding, and accepting of ourselves. It all starts here within you.

What will other people think? This fear is the sole reason why men, in particular, have such a difficult time connecting with the water element. I have observed that most of my male clients have difficulty moving with water. Not dancing—just *moving*. They are rigid and linear with not an ounce of flow in their bodies. Why? Movement like water is considered feminine. And for a long, long time, Western-cultured men have been told not to express themselves softly, physically or emotionally. They fear others will question their authority, manhood, and even their gender, sexuality, and identity as a whole. They fall into deluded thinking that women will stop being attracted to them because they might be seen as weak.

Everyone—regardless of gender—needs the water element for balance in their approach to themselves and life. Sometimes, the release of emotions comes in unhealthy ways (leading to a hole in the wall, shouting, or speeding down the road in a rage), rather than the more productive methods of verbalizing and expressing.

No matter your gender identity, *everyone* fears rejection. We all want to connect with others. In the primal survival view, without a community or tribe, you die. But for a healthy connection with others, you need to develop radical self-acceptance, self-nurturing, and self-respect first.

The water element helps to soften your approach to others and to yourself. Connection isn't healthy or positive when done from a place of lack, self-loathing, or revenge. These are facades for fear. So, if this is difficult for you, it is probably time to look back to your childhood and reflect on how your vulnerability was treated. And if you're a man who is scared that this somehow diminishes your masculinity or the way women perceive you, here's a study for you: women actually *prefer* emotionally mature men.[1] They feel safer, more willing to express themselves, and cared for, all of which prove that through humbleness and vulnerability, authentic connection can happen.

Creative Flow Exercise

If you're a writer, painter, dancer, or any creative experiencing a block, I challenge you. Put on some music that is sexy and central to you (something you deeply resonate with), slightly close your eyes, and focus internally. Begin to move. Sway with the music; let it move every part of your body like it is the blood nourishing it. Just move. No other directions.

You feel like moving your hips? Do it.

You feel shaking your head to the rhythm? Do it.

Want to jump up and down? Spin in circles? Move like a fish? Do it. Do it. Do it.

Think about softening all your joints and trying to move your body in ways you haven't done before. Sink your head into those visions entirely. Forget about your art. Forget your deadlines. Forget any anxiety you may have about other people's opinions. Empty your head.

Do this for the whole piece of music.

Feeling a little more relaxed?

Now, allow your art to flow without restrictions and judgment. Let it just flow out of you. No thoughts about form or structure or requirements. Allow the *flow* to take you where it needs to *go*. Your fear about fulfilling expectations and performing well—they're all slowing you down, blocking you. Let all these thoughts out. All you're doing now is channeling your artistic abilities, flowing freely, and creating unbelievable and important things.

You are water. Do you see how beautiful that is?

ASPIRE TO DESIRE

I hosted a retreat up in the mountains of East Tennessee inside a primitive retreat center complete with yurts, a half-indoor, half-outdoor kitchen and dining room, and a beautiful yoga shala. Everyone arrived on a Thursday, and that evening, we all set our intentions for the weekend.

Among those who signed up for the retreat were two Mormon ladies who were ready to let go of a lot of "stuff"—including their husbands. From a young age, they had been told that their purpose in life was to make babies and serve their husbands. Deep down, they felt frustrated because they could see there was more, but their future seemed inescapable.

Friday's theme was acknowledging and releasing, so we used the elements to release and ask, "What's not serving me? What can I let go?" We explored each element but concentrated on wood (releasing) and fire (burning away blocks and bringing in passion). There were many tears and breakthroughs for everyone, including me, that day. Then, in the evening, I asked each participant to write down the things that needed to be released for them to move on to an empowered and peaceful life. I created a fire ceremony to honor and witness each person's release.

For Saturday's theme, we all envisioned our lives again but *without* what held us back. Now what can we do? What are the new possibilities in our lives? What does our new life look like and feel like? It happened to be raining that day, which worked simultaneously with the qualities of water—the element we most closely focused on.

Surrounded by the sounds of rain pitter-pattering against the roof of the shala, I guided the class through flowy, syrupy movements, allowing our feelings to come up and be there. Softening our borders to accept something new and desired. Bringing this all in through circular, connected, sensual movement.

The two ladies started to blossom. Like watering a dried-up plant, their tears released years of frustration. In the fire ceremony the night before, they had expressed a desire for lovers. They wanted to embrace their sensuality, taboo in the culture they belonged to—surprising because, as one of the ladies told me, she had seven children, and despite that, at the age of 42, she was just beginning to discover pleasure and passion in sex.

After much movement and a future-visioning meditation, the ladies each had their own breakthrough and could actually imagine their new lives: a major shift in perspective, response to triggers, and execution of a plan. They were able to channel the essential water element within them, recognize their desires, and flow past all their regrets. For so long, they were captive to the thought, *What will my community think*? Finally, they broke free of shame and guilt, two pervasive emotions that erode and destroy the freedom of pursuit.

These two proved something that day: using the water element's qualities and the second chakra teachings, even the most repressed and rigid of us can make wiggle room for life's speed bumps and flow toward our desires.

Align with Water

Here are some resources that will help you align the water element within you and beyond you.

Water Spotify Playlist:

Move with Me Videos:

SHAKE IT OFF LIKE WOOD

WOOD 3rd Chakra: Solar plexus	Arrhythmic, chaotic, shake it out	Lean on your **bones**. Thrive in **structured chaos**. **Jiggle, giggle, and shake** off bad energy.	Clear your mind of unnecessary obstructions. Make way for new growth. Self-nurture.	Self-support

Have you ever felt like you're completely stuck in life? Like you just can't jump over the hurdle in front you, and there's an enormous burden weighing you down? You want to grow and nurture yourself and make way for new opportunities, but you just can't seem to push through all the experiences you've endured so far?

The process of acknowledging what's "stuck" is at the core of the wood element. By bringing into consciousness what limits you, makes you feel awful and oppressed, and causes you to perceive yourself as unworthy, you can *express* those burdens by physically and mentally shaking them off.

Wood is about letting go. Try it. Stand up and begin to think of all the obstacles stopping you from who you want to be and what you want to do. As you think of them, begin to shake, shake, shake, starting at your legs and slowly bringing that jiggling and shaking up and through your torso and into your head. Loosen your shoulders, shrug, and release. Imagine flinging off all the trauma and pressure and expectations like a tree that shakes in the wind, letting go of old, withered leaves. Shake and jiggle and giggle. Fill your heart with laughter. Wherever you have pain, soreness, or stiffness, bring an earthquake up and through these parts. As you slowly stop, notice how light you feel. How happy and confident. Notice your body—does it now feel like it's ready to move where you want to move, do what you want to do? At the very least, blood is now flowing.

In your day-to-day life, new challenges and pressures crop up like weeds. You can either let them grow all over the place and soak up all the nutrients the trees need, or you can pluck them out before they take root.

Imagine this. You're sitting at your desk, and your boss walks in, slams a stack of papers down, and angrily yells, "This is the worst crap I've ever seen!" When he storms out of the office, you have options: either stay frozen on the spot, not sure what to do next or how you can ever look him in the eyes again, or you can shake it off before it attacks your self-esteem, intentionally decide not to take on the emotional burden your boss just threw at you, and move on with your work.

Shaking it off is a great defense when something is coming at you. If you're constantly moving, nothing can stick. Cultural and societal pressures, in addition to traumas created from past events, may feel overbearing, but remember—they're uncontrollable. Yes, these pressures can cause people to feel wrong or unworthy. But again, no person has total authority over society's expectations, let alone the ability to influence the past. What you can control is your reaction to the expectations and the traumas. Acknowledge how awful the emotional weight feels, understand that it's an oppressive force, and then express it by letting go. Release the pressure, control, and pain. Uncontrollable situations are the norm in this world, but just as how a tree stays strong even in the face of winds and storms, so can you.

Wood is solid, dependable, adaptable, and can survive nearly anything. It continues to stand tall and grow, like the Great Basin bristlecone pine tree, which is 5,000 years old.

And what do trees do? Shake. They shake off old leaves to make place for new ones. They shed branches to grow stronger. They release the past to make way for the present and the future. When you practice the wood element, you replace pain, anxiety, and stuckness with the seeds of growth. Think of a tiny, green sprout surviving against all odds, pushing through the hard earth to make it out into the world by growing out of a crack in the concrete. That's wood—ever-growing determination.

Wood: Questions to Ask Yourself

- Do I support myself?
- Do I find humor in the silver linings?
- Do I believe in myself unconditionally?
- Do I stand up for myself?
- Do I recognize what needs to go and release it?

Remember the two Mormon ladies from the previous chapter? They both felt so stuck—emotionally, physically, and sexually—yet managed to free themselves by fully embracing the water element within them and bringing it to the forefront.

The next day, I taught them the technique of integrating these elements into their day-to-day lives. It's great to finally become aware of these elements and find the right rhythms to channel them forth, but only practicing movements within the confines of a retreat is not enough. It's the everyday living that needs the most attention.

I opened the floor for a heart-to-heart discussion: "What element do you think you will utilize the most in your lives from now on?"

One of the ladies, a beautiful 42-year-old, readied herself to answer. I predicted she would say water. The day before, she had connected with the element so deeply that she had had a visceral emotional reaction.

But when her turn came, she said, "I'm going to use wood."

"Why?" I asked, surprised.

"I already know that once I go back home, I'll be constantly approached by my family—husband, kids, relatives—all asking me, 'Why did you change?' or 'Why did you do that?' or 'You're not who you used to be.' And when that happens, I want to just shake it all off and not let their opinions stick. I want to set that boundary, and wood is going to help me with that."

I smiled. I should've known; whenever I told the group we were going to move with the wood element, she would get giddy with happiness. Turns out, she really enjoyed the chaotic, arrhythmic, earthquake movements similar to an all-out tantrum. These movements helped her release, put space between her and her triggers, and powerfully brought laughter to her challenges—which in turn removed the gravity of her difficulties.

As the retreat came to an end, I could see she had fully grasped the beauty of the wood element. Now that she had shaken things out of her tissues and into her consciousness, the next step was to continue shaking off all comments, complaints, and opinions that would stand in the way of reclaiming herself.

Wood provides a powerful, powerful structure. It is a system, a framework, for growth. Just as birch trees, tall and thin trees found in the mountains, can bend in all directions but not break, even when enduring the harshest of winds, you too can stay strong and centered despite your environment.

Humans are born with the same structure: bones. What are the first words out of someone's mouth when describing an old house, one that has withstood the test of time and harsh storms? "It has good bones."

Your bones support your body unconditionally. They have the same stability and tenacity.

Wood teaches that you don't require external support to stand straight. Everything you need already exists inside you, including the bones (the trunk of your tree) in your legs, arms, and back, which keep you upright and moving forward. Birch trees may be self-supporting, but they also move constantly. And that's because growth doesn't occur in stagnation; you need to move—physically and emotionally.

Move those bones. Bending your joints, even something as simple as bending your elbow, can help more synovial fluid enter the spaces between the bones, improving your flexibility and *releasing* what has been bottled for too long.

Moving physically will then help you move emotionally: by shaking off the weights that hold you back. A dead-end job or a relationship that isn't working out might be keeping you in the past, but by releasing these, you can move from a place where you're stuck to a new place that allows healing and growth.

The first step to this journey is the simplest but can often be the most difficult: you must recognize that you're stuck. For many of my clients, including the retreat ladies who did not feel well-equipped to face the challenges of their lives and relationships, the biggest adversity is recognizing when things just aren't working. They see some signs—they keep getting sick, have difficulty eating, or feel anxious. But it's only when they dig deep that they find out the root of the issue: a relationship, worry, or life event needs to be shaken off.

Wood Movement Exercise

Put this music on:

Let your head bob with this quirky, staccato, piano piece from Charlie Brown and your childhood. Take the head bob into your shoulders and let your shoulders and arms dance in non-syncopated, playful movements. Shrug off any stiffness, pain, and "should"s. Let your chest, waist, and hips bounce like an excited child. As you trickle down this rhythm (arrhythmia!) to your legs, separate the bones on the way down to your feet. Pretend you are on hot sand, and pick your feet up and down rapidly so they won't get burned. Let yourself laugh at your own silliness—I mean, belly laugh! Now, how do you feel?

MICHELLE'S STORY

Bringing awareness to the seed of old beliefs can help identify traumas, triggers, and areas of improvement, sure. But at the same time, it's vital to recognize that no one can change the past or the people in the past. Only the "now" can change future responses and outcomes.

After recognizing the weights you carry, the next step is to *do something about them*. I always encourage my clients to listen to that tiny voice inside them telling them to do "it," telling them to change. Yet, shifting directions is scary—after all, it could potentially impact not only one life but many. Plus, not everyone handles change well, especially when worrying about what other people think.

I had a client who, when she first came to me, was technically married to a man—but to me, it seemed more like she was really married to her job. Raising a daughter and working in a high-stress government job, "pressure" didn't even begin to describe what she was enduring day in and day out. Pushed to the absolute limit, the client, who I'll refer to as Michelle, never slowed down, never let up, and felt like she would break apart at any minute.

All of this stress came to a head when Michelle visited a nurse practitioner who ran some tests and reported, "You have severe adult-onset diabetes."

Her cortisol levels were soaring. Cortisol, a steroid hormone produced by the body's adrenal glands, is necessary in small amounts but can be dangerous in excess. The worst part, for Michelle, was the worry that if she was preoccupied with hospital visits or even, in the worst-case scenario, if she died as her grandmother had from the same condition, she wouldn't be around for her daughter.

When Michelle came to me with these concerns, the first course of action we took was addressing her nutrition, adding pancreas-supportive supplements to her diet. Then, we discussed increasing how much exercise she got, noting how more movement would reduce stress, get her blood pumping, and regulate her hormones.[1]

I prescribed another solution: she had to shut the world out once a week. No husband, no daughter, no work pressures, and not even her dog. She had to draw a hot bath with salts and essential oils to relax the muscles and the mind, light candles to put a visual to the relaxation, and sit in the bath for a minimum of 30 minutes. Her family could not bother her during this time, with the exception of a dire, life-threatening emergency. All of their needs had to wait until after Michelle's alone time.

The change in routine was not simple. Selflessness (and, as a result, self-neglect) had become so ingrained in her everyday life that even finding time for a short, once-a-week bath seemed like an insurmountable task. Michelle is not the only person I've worked with who felt this way. Many people find comfort in their pain, thinking it's easier to continue suffering than to do the work and find out who they are underneath the misery. The seemingly simple act of taking one step to break normal patterns is courageous. Never underestimate the all-powerful, all-consuming resistance to change. Michelle's willingness to put her life on pause and take a bath, though uncomplicated on the surface, was undoubtedly brave and daring.

It was this first bath that planted a seed for her. She could find time for herself. She could take a break. She could shed all those external worries and exist in her body, fully and uninterrupted, and the world didn't end. Even better, it showed that she wasn't a bad mother, wife, or employee for taking care of herself and her body's needs. This shift in perspective, she later discovered, would come to save her life. The ability to step off your rutted path to try something new and different is extremely edifying.

After a few weeks of this, Michelle's stress levels dropped, and her anger and mood swings diminished. She was able to handle her workload much easier and with a better attitude, all of which became motivators to keep going. In just six weeks, she returned to the doctor's office for more testing, and her original diagnosis had decreased in severity. With proven results, she became even more open to change and gained the momentum to continue down a path of self-preservation.

Michelle had a vision, a dream inspired by her grandmother who raised her and put her through school: she wanted to help financially stressed college students pay for books and supplies. Being the first to graduate from college in her family, Michelle remembered how her grandmother, affectionately known as "Nana," would always pull money out of a stashed-away envelope and give it to her whenever needed. Not all students have a Nana in their lives though, and Michelle wanted to assist them, knowing that financial aid can only cover so much.

Shrugging off the unnecessary worries that weighed her down, Michelle found room within herself for more confidence. Her desire to help these students turned into a successful organization that funds school supplies and necessities for students on financial aid. Her dream came true. She did away with what limited her (the self-sacrificing compulsion to care for everyone but herself) and instead manifested her thoughts into altruistic endeavors that met her need to nurture others while still leading to self-actualization.

In Michelle's words: "What was also key for me was connecting with another soul who wasn't mired in the chaos of my life and gave me perspective. Family members are in the thick of your drama and usually can't help you. Coworkers often stack their complaints and stress on top of yours, and you just end up rolling around in a pity party together. Too many people (women in particular) get bogged down with the negative tapes playing in their heads and stop believing in their abilities. Positive energy and beliefs were key to my progress."

The wood element empowers you to shake off the external judgment, the cobwebs, and stand by your decision to change, to follow the path that brings you delight and happiness. Judgment tightens and restricts you, and the wood element says, "Break the shackles of judgment. Live unrestricted."

Just as a tree sheds its leaves when the time comes, you too will know when it's time to move on. You will feel it in your gut, in your solar plexus, that something just isn't working out anymore. Don't ignore that intuition—it's a sign that you're no longer nourished, happy, or moving forward.

Stress is a killer. And it's only one example of a negative emotion to be discarded and replaced. You never know; shaking off a challenge could potentially save your life one day, maybe in more ways than one.

Symptoms of Disconnect with Wood

- Irritable Bowel Syndrome (IBS)
- Abnormal/excessive weight gain or loss
- Ulcers
- Diabetes
- Issues in pancreas, liver, or colon
- Heartburn
- Eating disorders
- Low self-esteem and confidence

GUT FEELING

Wood is related to your third chakra, known as *Manipura* or *Nabhi* in Sanskrit, and is located in the solar plexus, your abdomen, the energy center for the self. The solar plexus is where you derive *power*. It's like when you throw a punch—all the weight behind it comes from a durable and sturdy foundation at your core. The inner strength found here is the reason why, when I walk into a room, I always lead with my chest: arms to the side, solar plexus out, and head held high with good posture. When I was younger and making a name for myself, I had the confidence to be the loudest, smartest, and most engaged person in the room, no matter where I was. Other people's reactions proved me right: they would unconsciously stop, stare, and soon come over to me to talk and make connections. To carry yourself with gravitas like this, you need to strengthen your solar plexus—that's where your sense of purpose, identity, self-confidence, and individuality lies.

The third chakra is also where your stomach is located. This is where you experience hunger and the need to nourish. Do you need to eat more? Do you eat too much? Are you craving sugar? Salt? Ayurveda practice encourages a diet of six *rasas*, or tastes: sweet, sour, salty, pungent, bitter, and astringent. Each taste impacts the *doshas*, Vata, Kapha, and Pitta. Over-indulging in salty foods, in particular, pacifies Vata, but it aggravates Pitta and Kapha, creating an imbalance.[2] Vata is associated with air, Pitta embodies fire, and Kapha is characterized by water. All three doshas exist in everyone, but their levels are unique to each individual. So, paying attention to the signs your body presents can help you specifically address the dosha you are lacking or have in excess.

I crave salty, crunchy potato chips and could eat an entire bag of them if I allowed it. However, such intense cravings are massive warning signs from the body that there's something askew. An overwhelming, stressful environment may deplete you of all energy—which is when you are likely to crave sweet, sour, and salty tastes, in an effort to calm Vata and regain equilibrium. But just because these tastes soothe Vata doesn't mean they won't flare up Pitta and Kapha, leading to even more feelings of anger, crankiness, and irritability.[3] Everything requires balance, even the foods you eat and how much you consume.

Thankfully, your physical body strives for this balance, homeostasis, whether you are conscious of it or not. Just as you can shrug off emotional worries and pains, the digestive system can absorb the nutrients necessary for growth and let go of anything unnecessary as waste.

Doing this work psychologically, however, is not part of your autonomic nervous system—meaning, it requires intention. It's necessary to listen closely to what your body is saying, to understand what trauma or ingrained behaviors have settled deeply into your tissues. There are so many feelings that originate in the stomach, including tightness, nausea, pleasure, deprivation, knots, fullness, and emptiness. As mentioned, even the very act of craving a particular food can give you insight into what your body is lacking and what emotions you're experiencing. The third chakra is where you nourish and nurture yourself, so deep patterns are embedded here.

With all the collective experience that resides in the third chakra, it's only natural that your intuition forms here as well. It's called a *gut* feeling for a reason.

"I have a good feeling about this."

"I have a bad feeling about this place."

"I have a feeling I will not enjoy this."

"My gut says this opportunity is not for me."

There is so much insight here! When you make decisions, you may be swayed by social pressures, expectations, or perceived rewards. But your gut tells the truth. It reveals your innermost feelings.

Only through this process will you be able to adequately discern what to hold on to and what to let go. Your solar plexus can help you find answers to questions like "How much freedom do I have in the matter?" or "Is it possible to change the situation?" or "Is this fixable?" Sometimes, the answer is no. That's when you accept your lack of control and . . . *shake it off*.

Don't revert back to old, reflexive behaviors. Instead, work the muscle. Keep working on the new thought, the new behavior. The lack of attention to the old behavior will atrophy the old thoughts and pathways, just as it does when you stop using a muscle in your body. Trust your intuition to tell you what the right behaviors and changes are, and continue working on them. The more you work those muscles and bones, the stronger they grow. The stronger they grow, the better your solar plexus will be at discerning the situations you find yourself in, and the better the wood element will support you to cast aside unnecessary weight.

Wood Affirmations

- I am amused by myself.
- I shake off my negative thoughts and feelings.
- My self-doubt drops like dead leaves in the fall.
- I let go of the "should"s weighing on my shoulders.
- I delight in myself.

SHAKE "SHOULD"S FROM THE SHOULDERS

I had always been an athletic child, but when I was in first grade, my parents told me I should try to do something in the arts. I was six and had no idea what I wanted, so I asked them to pick something for me instead. Since my mom was a piano player, they picked the piano. I diligently took piano lessons for six years. And I absolutely hated it.

Sitting still was not one of my strengths; that had never been my way of expression. I needed to move and sway and jump, not sit and press keys. It took me a long, long time to acknowledge that piano was a major block in my road. I mean, every time I played a wrong note, my self-esteem would plummet. It sucked all of the energy out of me, but even once I knew that, quitting was difficult. Finally, I broke down and told my parents there was no way I could play the piano.

Quitting piano opened up time in my day, and I followed a friend's suggestion to take modern dance with her. The minute the music came on, I found I was a natural and felt so completely comfortable in class. I felt confident in my body. I was able to finally express all that I was feeling, and dancing just felt so . . . right. I instinctively took my frustrations as a 14-year-old girl navigating high school and expressed them through my movements. It strengthened my intuition, confidence, and self-awareness. To think I could've been doing this much earlier!

This is what the wood element is about: shedding the negative energy that holds you back and freeing yourself to experience new growth . . . and not taking "it" too seriously.

Once I began dancing, I never stopped. It became my primary medium of expression. Even those emotions I couldn't put into words found a way to flow out of me through movements. I danced through high school and college. During my senior year of college, I had a vision: a dance involving a person wrestling with their past and future. On a journey of self-learning (as most people are when they're in college), I wanted to embody my struggle and express how, even though I experienced feelings of uncertainty, I still continued down a path of discovery.

Two of my friends accompanied me, one dancing as my past self and the other as my future self, and together, the three of us performed—the intense emotions that flung off of us were simply incredible. The past, like a never-ending lurking shadow, pulled me back; the future enticed me forward; and in the middle, I danced my heart out. I shook off the past, the emotions, old ways of thinking, and restrictive habits, and I branched out toward my future. I released everything, even experiences and feelings I never even knew were hidden in the very depths of my being.

I called the dance "Trimages" for the three images on stage. For this performance, one of my friends, Parker (who danced as "future me"), wrote a song to go along with the movements. It coincided beautifully with the piano music performed by Kristen Waskowitz Woods and truly captured the very essence of the dance.

· · · · · · · ·

Letting Go
Written by Parker

As I look into the mirror
My past unfolds a shadow
A never-ending memory of a life long ago

Should I stay in my shadow
Taunting me into its realm
Or escape to the future
Reflected in the glass

This conflict inside me
I cannot seem to escape
My future
My past
Try to make me whole
I'm empty

I look into my soul
To seek the individual
Which grows within

I see myself inside the mirror
I am myself inside the mirror
I am myself
And all I have is myself

As I look into the mirror
My past unfolds a shadow
A never-ending memory
Of a life so long ago

I'm letting go . . .

. . . .

Align with Wood

Here are some resources that will help you align with the wood element within you and beyond you.

Wood Spotify Playlist:

Move with Me Videos

CHAPTER FIVE
AS PASSIONATE AS FIRE

FIRE 4th Chakra: Heart	Pumping, rhythmic, moving to the beat	Get your **heart pounding**. Let the **rhythm move you.**	Tap into your desires. Fuel your passion. Release anger. Be unstoppable.	Self-love

In the world of human innovation, fire has been touted as the greatest of all—it essentially sowed the seed for everything mankind has grown into today. Since the time of ancestors, humans have evolved with an ingrained deep connection to fire: it protects from the cold, cooks food, lights the way forward, gathers communities, and unconditionally shares warmth and safety.

Ancient Vedic texts introduce the fire element as *Anahata*, the heart chakra. In Sanskrit, *Anahata* means unhurt, unstruck, and unbeaten. It is the center of love and compassion—feelings you hold toward yourself and others.[1] The heart is filled with *Chitta*, or the ability to feel, and when this *Chitta* blossoms in a positive direction, positive feelings abound.[2] Fire is the beating heart of the body where life erupts and why, symbolically, the heart is associated with love, desire, compassion, anger, and passion. It's often considered a bridge that connects the lower and higher energies of being—a place that is free, independent, and self-fulfilling. However, if the *Chitta* accumulates toward negativity, you experience increasing feelings of anger and hostility.

Apart from the heart, fire also concerns the lungs, liver, thymus, and blood. Any time you move your body or exercise, whether lifting weights, jogging, or dancing, you can likely "feel the burn" of fire. When your heart beats faster, your blood pumps faster, fanning the flames within. Think of someone you love or someone who loves you. Picture the warmth and love that turns your knees into jelly. Your heart may feel so full it could explode. If you haven't already, switch your thoughts to a romantic partner or someone you have a crush on. Let in those sexy thoughts, and feel yourself blush. Burn with desire. Do you feel passion rising in you yet?

The same fire that entices intense, heated feelings is also inflamed at the thought of other relationships. Think of your child or your pet being attacked. Do you feel a tide of anger and protectiveness wash over you? Do you feel like storming over and saving them?

That's fire too. Fire protects. Fire loves. Fire fights.

And fire heals, burning away bad energy and toxicity by allowing you to set boundaries—with others and yourself. Ever had a bad habit you wanted to break? Maybe you smoke two packs a day, or you're always running late, or you lose your temper at the slightest inconvenience. To quit these habits, you need the element of fire to burn away negativity and fuel your passion about the new goals and standards you set for yourself. Set those flames to release anything and everything that does not serve you (consciously or unconsciously).

Try it! Go all the way. Say to yourself, "I will quit smoking" or "I'll get to where I need to be 10 minutes sooner" or "I'll keep the fire within burning low and stop throwing a tantrum." Sure, you might slip up once or twice, but when you do, remind yourself of the pledge you made to your heart, in your heart—and keep it. Because when the heart (the organ that coordinates with your veins to reach every crack and crevice of your body) gets involved, your whole life is affected.

Fire: Questions to Ask Yourself

- Do I love myself?
- Am I connected to my desires and passions?
- Do I feel like I am one big hot button?
- Am I motivated?

As with other elements, too much and too little fire can spell disaster and chaos; except, with fire, an imbalance may manifest more clearly and noticeably. Fire affects your entire life force, so when there's a mismatch, you feel it deeply.

It makes sense, then, that blocked fire results in anger, inciting a fierce, combustible feeling. Think of how you feel when you're angry. Do you suddenly feel hot? Even if you can't see yourself, can you feel all the blood rushing to your face, turning your ears and cheeks bright red? This is the experience of too much fire—destructive and disruptive.

On the flipside, think of how you feel in the dark, cold months of winter. You probably experience some breathing issues—maybe a bad cold or cough—and feel a lot more lethargic and sadder than usual. The fire element in you is on its low embers. There's too little. Why do you think seasonal depression is so rampant during winter? The lack of sunlight leaves your internal fire un-stoked.

Fire is my favorite element and one I connect with the most—but that doesn't mean taming the fire within came easy to me. In fact, I struggled with it the most! I was born under the astrological sign, Aries, which is driven by fire and the red planet of Mars. People with this sign tend to be impulsive, fiery, and hot-headed, and they're always the first to jump into any situation. No fear. Just fierce.

Growing up, these characteristics fed my adrenaline addiction and the uncontrollable push to take on any challenge. All it would take was one "I dare you to," and I would feel my blood run hot and rush to my head, taking over my body until I did whatever I'd been challenged to do. To say I have been motivated in my life is a gross understatement. Like a raging lion on a hunt, I have pushed myself to accomplish milestones and reach higher and higher goals. The name for people like me in the 80s was "megalomaniac," and I was just that! The only caveat is that people with high fire like me also burn out—and burn out hard.

As an executive at Coca-Cola, I had 2,500 accounts in the San Fernando Valley of California. Every morning, I would be up at 6 a.m., slamming back coffee and communicating with our headquarters in Atlanta. After paperwork and prep for the day, I'd leave around 10 a.m. to hit as many accounts as possible—which was every kind of restaurant imaginable—all before lunch. Competing with eight other representatives, I attempted to sign up the most restaurants for Coca-Cola products, which also proved difficult and anxiety-inducing due to the irreverent competition with PepsiCo in my area. On top of all that, I attempted to earn my MBA at night school at Pepperdine University. A top producer for my region while making all As in school, sleeping about four hours a night, and working on weekends, I burned the candles at both ends *and* in the middle!

But here's the other side of the coin: some days, I just couldn't force myself to leave my apartment. Exhausted, depleted, and depressed, I assumed something was very wrong with me. My manager would point me out in employee reviews and remark that when I was "on fire," I was untouchable competitively. But when I "disappeared" for days, my numbers dropped. My performance was inconsistent. My spark often fizzled out, leaving behind the acrid smoke of an over-stoked fire. My motto back in those days was to "party as hard as I worked." I simply had no balance. I was a "disco queen" back then and used the hours of dancing and drinking as my creative outlet and stress relief. It was how I balanced the intensity and drive of the working part of my life with the intensity of the wild side of my life—all fun until the day I was pregnant and it all halted abruptly for the following two years while I had my boys. Subsequently, it took me a solid year to break my adrenaline addiction and say no to dares, caffeine, and stimulants that I had unhealthily relied on for so long. I committed to healing, to realigning my habits and bodily needs, and it changed everything. Now, because I recognize how important this harmony is for my body and mindset, I am able to control the fire in my blood and bring stability to my heart, even when "dared" to do otherwise.

> ## Symptoms of Disconnect with Fire
>
> *Too much fire:*
>
> - High temperature and flushing red in the face or parts of the body
> - Feeling dehydrated all the time
> - Dry, flaky skin
> - Heartburn and high blood pressure
> - Feeling perpetually angry, on edge, and ready to explode with very little triggering
> - Feeling routinely stressed
> - Uncontrollably driven
>
> *Too little fire:*
>
> - Feeling cold all the time and clammy hands
> - Lung and breathing issues
> - Lack of drive, passion, and motivation
> - No vim or vigor
> - Inability to express compassion
> - Experiencing lethargy and depression

HOT BLOODED

While trying to grow WildHeart Expressive, I took on a business partner, who I'll call Emma.

I met Emma at a screenplay writing group. When she heard I wanted to start my own somatic movement company to help people get out of their minds and into their bodies, she was sold. It was her, after all, who first questioned me about why I dropped dancing and somatic therapy if it gave me so much joy in the past. From the moment I told her I wanted to re-enter the space, she sounded excited about my idea and promised she could help me build my online business. The idea of running the business on my own seemed tough. With so many factors at play, I could use some help, so I thought, *Why not*? And I let her in.

With time, it became clear that we were a mismatch. She pushed me to extremes, and I struggled to keep up, all because I didn't keep a handle on my fire. My overachieving nature burned hotter than ever, and my ego grew with images of grandeur and success. My heart was beating fast and my head was spinning, and once again, I fell into the trap of doing too much, of burning so bright, that I met a familiar fate: burnout.

Ego is fire—too much and it blazes out of control.

My tiny spark of wanting to help people blazed into an unchecked wildfire of achieving uber success. I became unfocused, untamed, and undisciplined. At the end of the line, it was simply unsustainable. I hemorrhaged money while also completing a hundred other tasks Emma told me to do, all for the "sake" of the company.

Eventually, understanding dawned on me. Yes, I was driven and passionate about my business, but what I experienced in the moment was a bad kind of drive. It was the kind that burns bright and just as quickly gets snuffed out. I came to a realization: my heart and lungs were tired, my mind was completely overwhelmed, and I had to pull the plug. It was time.

Of course, I was angry. I had let my fire (ego) take over my life, and I was completely worn out. It would have been easy for me to take it out on Emma, to yell at her for pushing me . . . but what was the point? It was my own inability to control my fire that had brought me here, no matter what or who the catalyst was. After some reflection, I decided that the best way for me to move forward was to heal. I needed to put space between us—me, the business, and

Emma—ASAP. I stopped the out-of-control train, stepped off, and let it go on without me. In doing that, I faced failure, incompetency, my falsely fed ego, and extreme vulnerability. I was numb, not fully understanding how I got here, and perplexed about what to do next. So, I decided to sequester away from everything and do nothing—a reset. This was a huge challenge and something I had never before done in my whole life. Looking back, I think I was exceedingly driven from the moment I could walk!

As the healing process took place, I was waking up early with the sun in the mornings, walking around my house, and seeing what needed to be done; going on a run with my dogs; immersing myself in paddleboarding; and simply having fun. Of course, I eventually picked up WildHeart Expressive again but, this time, on my own terms. I did it for me, according to what I wanted out of it, not what someone else told me I should aim for. My fire was now more intimate and personal, driven from *my* heart. And it all happened because I confronted my ego, identified the part that craved everyone's approval, and released its hold on me. I set boundaries that allowed me to find and follow my passion. As the fire in me calmed and integrated, my creativity exploded. WildHeart Expressive grew and grew, and before long, I was doing exactly what I wanted to do with my business: simply help people understand who they are.

Notice how easy it was for my emotions to burn out of control? That's because I was so seduced by the "fast track to fame and fortune" and overly passionate about the idea that I let the fire in me grow unguided and unchecked. Both passion and anger depend on fire to fuel it, but in both cases, when you're focused on a facade, you end up doing more harm than good. But there is a way to guide your inner fire to allow beauty to emerge—a way to turn your anger (your "piss and vinegar") into passion and your passion into creativity.

I call this process *alchemical redirection*.

To engage in alchemical redirection, you have to be conscious of your triggers. What causes you to explode in rage? What makes you so angry that you can't even talk? Identify these triggers and redirect all that fire and energy into a passionate pursuit. I used to have days when it felt like I was perpetually at a boiling point. Back when I was in certain relationships, every interaction with my partner would leave me doused in red-hot fire. I would be so angry that I could have chewed through steel! But instead of staying in an angry, disempowered state, I would force my mind to redirect the energy. My group movement classes were a blessing during those days. My desire to be present for the participants and their needs helped me leave those intense, distracting feelings at the studio door, and I could just channel all that rage and fire into movement, dance my way through expression, and create something beautiful out of all the negativity. Other times, I would redirect my mind to other creative pursuits like rearranging my bookshelves, decorating my living room, or searching for the perfect birthday present for my kids. You can find any pursuit that works for you, creative or not. The main purpose of redirection is to change the target of your drive and energy from the uncontrollable trigger (in my case, my partner) to a situation or project you *can* control. By focusing and directing your inner fire toward something you can affect, you can see and experience a positive product, and in the process, you transform your rage into creative passion.

Don't think too hard about it! Do what feels natural to you. If you're feeling so angry you could scream, then just scream into a pillow. Take out your journal, and scribble out every curse word. Call a good friend and vent. Grab your partner and make passionate love! My favorite exercise to do is writing my feelings and triggers on a piece of paper, setting it on fire, and watching it quickly reduce to a pile of ashes. Once that paper is gone, so is my anger. It's similar to slash-and-burn agriculture—you burn down a field of crops so it can nourish the soil, making way for fresh growth in the new season. When I burn down the thoughts that make me angry, I feel so light and in control that I could do anything.

FLAMBÉ

One of the best qualities of the fire element is its ability to burn away toxic connections you may be holding onto (or ones that are holding onto you). Fire has saved me, time and again, from bad, negative relationships that weighed me down. One of these relationships, in particular, was my connection to alcohol.

I grew up in a family of cocktailers. My parents believed that as soon as the clock struck five, the liqueurs and the mixers and the shakers had to come out. This was such a habit in our home that even when we took a road trip, my little self, in the backseat of our car, would put together a quick cocktail and pass it to my parents in the front as soon as the five o'clock bell rang! Immersed in such a cultural background, drinking was not only a natural part of my social life but a big part of my overall life. And when the COVID-19 pandemic hit, my desire to drink became much more frequent.

Tequila being my drink of choice, I could easily knock back three or four cocktails a day. For me, the impulse didn't even come from the alcohol itself. I just liked the creative act of mixing different liquors and ingredients to create something delicious.

For many years, the role of alcohol in my life scratched away at the back of my mind. I began questioning my need for it. A couple of times, I even tried to cut down a bit, but eventually, I always slipped and bounced back to my regular patterns. Old habits die hard. But see, alcohol never caused me consistent problems. I never got so drunk that I would pass out (although, since alcohol stokes fire, I would occasionally rise up and become pretty caustic in an argument). The haze after those occasional benders left me feeling bad and anxious, not clear of what all went on. My body and joints were inflamed, and my mind was foggy and dull since alcohol is a depressant. The routine became less and less desirable, yet the habit of drinking and living with the impulsive daily triggers of wine pairings, signature cocktails, fancy martinis with the girls, and fine tequila on the rocks was stronger than my need to say no. Until one day.

Tailgate parties are huge in Knoxville, Tennessee, especially when it comes to University of Tennessee football. In broad daylight, usually in the stadium's parking lot before a game, bands play live music behind cars, people (some with their faces and bare chests painted orange and white) throw back beers and liquor of all kinds, and others play cornhole, a Southern game involving hacky sacks and wooden boards with holes cut out of them. One afternoon, my friends and I went tailgating before a UT football game, walking around with a few Bloody Marys and enjoying the party.

All in all, I only had about three drinks—no more than I usually do—and as the game started, we headed home to watch it on TV. We walked up a hill, and as we reached the top, I collapsed on the sidewalk. I just crumpled like one of those dolls that buckle at the knees and ragdolled onto the ground. I had blacked out—this had never, in all my years of drinking, happened to me before. My friend tried to support me and help me stand up, but all I could do was hold on and try to walk. Nothing made sense. I blacked out again on the way to the car. I made it safely back to my condo where I crashed face down on the couch. I slept for four hours straight, woke up at six in the evening, went to our food court downstairs, bought a double cheeseburger, inhaled it, and crashed again, only to wake up the next morning at eight o'clock.

When I woke up, I couldn't even believe the incidents of the day before. During that whole sequence of events, I had also fallen down a couple of times, injuring my tailbone. As I recovered, all I could think about was how stupid I had been to let harm befall my body, especially since, as a somatic movement coach, it's so important to my livelihood. But more than anything, I felt shame for having been irresponsible and disrespectful to my body.

Later, when I talked to my friends on the phone, they told me that I didn't seem like I had gone overboard. Someone even threw in the possibility that I was drugged or roofied. Absolutely shattering. Devastating enough to put anger and disgust between me and the "need" for alcohol. The words that surfaced for me were: "This is such unbecoming behavior, especially at your age and stature."

During the previous 10 years, I abstained from alcohol for dietary reasons but had not summoned the courage (another fire element) to take it out of my life for good. Reflecting, I realized that the habit likely stemmed from a place of cultural pressure. Like I said, I grew up in a family of cocktailers where you were considered just plain weird if you said no to a drink. I had to unlearn the behavior and go back to the very first time I drank alcohol. What was my "why" then? I put space between me and my habit so

I could create a mental shift and replace the cultural and social drive with a new desire for no alcohol at all. My brain needed to be trained; no alcohol would be the new norm.

I was definitely motivated to see this through, having noticed for some time that my body experienced certain symptoms whenever I had an extra drink or two—bloating, weight gain, joint inflammation, brain fog, and sometimes even psychological signs, such as a lack of motivation, negativity, or new rifts in my relationship with my partner. The negative erosive and oppressive effects of alcohol far outweighed the impulsive reflexive reach for a drink, yet I still struggled with my inner saboteur whenever I tried to turn down a "party cocktail." But deciding right then, I knew my experience and resolve would be different this time.

The following weekend, I led a three-day retreat in the mountains. After setting our intentions for the weekend on the first day, the participants and I specifically focused on what was holding us back from reaching our potential. The desire to drink seemed like an immediate and obvious option for me. I just needed to take choice out of the equation by cutting the ties to my desire.

That evening, I had a chance to make my new resolution gravely official—in the form of a sacred fire ritual. Allow me to state that rituals help solidify emotional, mental, and spiritual ideas and ideals. The mere act materializes the feelings and desires to change, like honing steel. On a piece of paper, I wrote one simple request: to release my *desire* to drink. The rest of my participants wrote about their courageous desires for change in their lives. Clutching the folded papers, we circled the fire and acknowledged its power. When I walked up to the fire, I was nervous, I'll admit it. My choice would finally be official, with witnesses to hear my fear and to support me. Once the paper burned,

I'd no longer be "trying" to quit drinking; I'd lose the desire for alcohol, period.

In the presence of intense heat, I could feel the fear in my flesh burn away. Walking as close as I could to the flames, I stated my wishes, threw the paper in the fire, and watched my habitual desire turn to ash. Feeling heavy and light at the same time, I reclaimed power for myself in a profound moment. I was so overwhelmed I even cried, having needed relief for a long, long time. I made a profound statement to myself: my well-being comes first, before cultural and social opinions, pressures, and habits.

Today, I am the queen of mocktails. As mentioned, my favorite part of drinking was not alcohol itself per se; I enjoyed the creativity that went into making the drinks. So, I still make delicious concoctions, just minus one ingredient. And you know what? I don't miss it. My fire still glows bright, and my body feels so healthy.

Rituals hold power. While prayers and wishes state the desired, a ritual embodies the emotions that mentally bug you, inserting space in between so you can look at them, examine them, and let them go. For example, one of the rituals I did to cleanse my aura of all the anger and regret I felt toward my ex-husband was using a ball of yarn and unlacing it slowly. I started at one corner of my room and started lacing it around objects and all around me, envisioning that each length of yarn was being laced right back through me. Each of these lengths was an energetic connection I had with him, pulling on my heart, stoking the fire. Slowly, I began systematically cutting through them one by one. With each snap of the scissors, I felt the release of tangled energy and toxic hooks that had connected him to me. I rolled all the cuttings into a ball and burned it. And if that wasn't enough, I buried the ashes. The fire burned any connection with him and put space and positive energy back where it had been missing, cleaning my aura of toxicity. Rituals, like these and more, have freed me.

Fire Affirmations

- I am passionate about my dreams and pursuits.
- My desires drive me.
- I connect to the rhythm of life.

DEAR "JOHN"

Just as love begins at the heart, so does hate. Sometimes, people direct a lot of hate toward themselves; maybe they're dissatisfied with who they are, how they look, or the way they behave. I'm sure you have, at least once in your life, looked into the mirror and hated what you saw. Maybe you've thought, *I'm such an idiot* or *Oh my God, here I go again.* Just because everyone experiences it, though, doesn't mean it's okay.

Where's the compassion? Imagine a friend saying all these things about themselves. What would you do? If you're a good friend, I bet you would jump in and immediately defend them from themselves. You would probably say, "No, you're beautiful, smart, and everyone enjoys your company!" See this forgiveness you have for your friend? How your fire burns a little brighter to protect them? Extend that kindness to yourself. You deserve to protect yourself. Find your fire and envelop it around you, creating a warm blanket, a warm hug. Do you feel loved? Do you feel self-assured? Do you feel that your own compassion will now support you through thick and thin? That's fire—you don't always have to direct it outward; directing it inward toward yourself and your body is one of the best ways to channel your heart chakra.

When you do eventually extend the compassion beyond yourself to others, give them grace. Say you notice a friend doing something that you strongly disapprove of. Instead of hating them for it or getting angry and yelling, pause. Acknowledge that you're not the same person as them. If you're able to create separation and space between you two (as in knowing where you end and they begin), you'll be able to observe their behavior without it yanking you up and down with their emotions. You may think, *Wow, they're making a lot of mistakes*, but add this to your thought: *They must be going through a learning curve.*

The minute you separate your energy from others and refrain from making their problems about you, you'll be able to watch them make mistakes and lend empathy, rather than blowing up on them. Just let them be, knowing their actions are not a reflection of you or your friendship. And while they can work themselves into a lather all they want, don't let anyone offload their stress onto you. Allow them to self-destruct. This is where you allow fire to protect you. Remember, you're no scratching post. Once they've released their own fire and need someone who loves them, then you can be there with your arms wide open.

Compassion Meditation Exercise

Close your eyes, and picture someone you absolutely detest. Someone who fans the flames of your anger. The feeling can be so intense that it makes you want to take action just to relieve the steam building up within you like a pressure cooker. It is at this moment that alchemical redirection can happen.

Admit that your greatest desire is to have peace in your heart and not a burning hatred. The path to peace is compassion. Again, put space between you and this person and their actions, and look at them from a different perspective. Think about how horrible they must feel about themselves to project such appalling behavior toward you. This perspective takes you out of the equation and gives the piss and vinegar back to them. Sometimes, "the only winning move is not to play."[3] Truly happy people don't do dreadful things to others. The greater the scale of the horrendous behavior, the greater their inner war is. It's not easy; believe me, I know. But still, I urge you to find a crumb of mercy because, when you do this, you convert that angry fire to compassion, even pity, and you can walk away with no attachment to that person or their actions. You feel so much lighter. You gain control.

Here's an example: I was in a two-year relationship with a newly divorced man. Since the very beginning, I knew that I was his rebound, and I made it clear that I wanted nothing serious with him. Despite this, he bombarded me with endless texts, phone calls, and dates, telling me he loved me and wanted me to move in with him. Somehow, he managed to persuade me, and I finally thought, just maybe, he really was serious about me. Recovering from knee reconstruction surgery around Valentine's Day, I drove to his house and hobbled around on my crutches to make a meal for him and his kids. Then, I left to allow him to spend the rest of the weekend with his family. I didn't think much of it—until I got a call from his sister.

She inquired about the whereabouts of her brother, and I told her that he was having dinner with their parents. Her voice was furious as she informed me that he was, in fact, with another woman he had been secretly seeing.

Shaken, I texted him, called him out on it, and told him I knew. Yes, he confirmed, he was seeing someone else behind my back.

I was angry. Pissed. I had told him not to drag me into something serious, but he did. Then, he betrayed the trust he worked so hard to earn.

As you can imagine, I had many things I wanted to say to him. Instead, I simply laid down the law: "Don't call me. Don't text me. We're done."

I realized that any negative feelings you carry for someone just keep you connected to them. They might do something to hurt you, but they can't make you angry. How you respond is on you. How you feel about it is still *your* decision. If they stoke the fire within you, then you're handing over control, and you'll continue to feel triggered. I did not want to give him control.

So, I rose above the horrible thing he did to me and decided that he was an immature man—a man who I could only pity. I chose to extend compassion to him, writing him a kind letter:

Dear John,

My emotions are still very raw around our relationship. It is horrible what you have done to my heart and to us. We spent most of our time and energy focused on building trust. We built our relationship on a foundation of open and honest communication, but your actions have shattered this over and over again. I gave you several opportunities to be honest, yet you lied continuously to be with her while telling me you wanted to have only me and marry me. Because I loved you, I bought your lies and, in turn, suffered your actions.

Therefore, there is nothing you can say at this point that will change anything. The relationship ended on the night of Valentine's Day, when I had confirmation of your behavior I had suffered through for two solid months. Two of the hardest months in my life, when you combine struggles with my mother's health, business finances, and my own surgery. You dishonored me and what we built.

I didn't see this coming. You could have at least saved our friendship with truth. Now, there is nothing left, and I am grieving the loss of love, trust, and dreams of a future together. I had a special place for you in my heart. That place is closed up and sacred now—full of good memories, healing, and positive lessons. You are not who I thought you were, and I have no problem saying goodbye to the person you are now.

I wish you well. I wish you happiness. I wish you confidence and security from within. I hope you love yourself someday. It sucks being where you are. I feel for you.

I leave you gently with love in my heart.

Be well.

Do well.

Love,
Angel

I released him with love and light, which gave him nothing to fight against.

I believe that if you throw a fireball at someone, you just give them an excuse to defend themselves and throw one back at you. Instead, with love and compassion, you can sever your ties with them. You may sometimes regret choosing meanness. But you'll never regret being kind.

RAGE IN A CAGE

During my divorce, I performed and traveled with the West African dance troupe Djoliba Don. Truly, one of the best decisions I've ever made. I was angry a lot back then, but all that pumping, moving up and down to the deafening beats of the drums, and foot-stomping incinerated the anger and drained the boiling resentment out of me through sweat. It bears repeating: express what's oppressed. There's no point in keeping all the madness and rage locked inside of you. Do something physical and exert your body to sweat, pump your heart, and breathe heavily. Put on music with drums and a deep beat, and just dance!

We've all been there: sometimes, even if we want to move, our bodies don't. I've seen this particularly in one of my male clients. He suffered from chronic lower back and hip pain. He would show up at my studio, and we would work together to release some of this pain through a Pilates machine for stretching. His joints were screaming! He was as stiff and inflexible as his own mentality and judgemental view of himself, which meant he didn't extend compassion or flexibility to others easily either. Every time he saw someone else, he had something negative to say:

"Would you look at her gold tooth?"

"What's with the purple hair?"

"He's put on a bit of weight, huh?"

If, as a kid, you ever took a magnifying glass in the sun and watched a spark erupt in the grass, then you know the power of concentrated fire. My client's ceaseless jabs at others seemed to scream, "Pay attention to me! Aren't I so much better than everyone else?" But really, the external reflected the internal. He wanted to shine a spotlight on other people's insecurities, in the hopes no one would notice his own. Constantly frustrated and mad at his own body, all that anger caused his in*flam*mation, keeping him stuck, recycling the disappointment he felt in himself. The frustrating part is that if he could have just loosened up his fixed mindset, his body might have followed the new energetic trend and loosened up too. The first step on this path is to be unconditionally compassionate and accepting of *yourself*.

There's a fire within you. Like with every element, it's all a balancing act. Once you embrace the embers, you can channel the fire any way you want. If your fire is just an ember, accelerate it with your focused passion and drive. On the other hand, remember that when you feel like a raging, destructive wildfire, you can master its enormous power and potential with love and compassion. It is the love in your heart that governs your fire, that directs it where *you* want.

Align with Fire

Here are some resources that will help you align with the fire element within you and beyond you.

Fire Spotify Playlist:

Move with Me Videos:

CHAPTER SIX
AIR "IT" OUT

AIR 5th Chakra: Throat	Verbal and physical expression, using breath to inspire and move	**Express** yourself. Use your **voice**. Enjoy your **breath**.	Use movement, words, and sounds to release your emotions. Release what is oppressed. Feel relief.	Self-respect

Imagine this: you're feeling angry at your partner for not calling you back immediately. Of course, the rational part of your brain knows that they could be busy, didn't happen to check their phone, or are in the middle of a conversation with someone else. But despite knowing this, you still feel uncontrollable anger bubble up inside you.

Why? What lies at the heart of this emotion?

Fear. Fear is usually the foundation of our negative emotions.

The fear of never being able to get up after a breakdown.

The fear that, by expressing, you'll only hurt yourself more.

The fear of what other people will think of you. In other words, *rejection*.

More often than not, ingrained fears result from moments when you have felt powerless or socially unsafe, commonly first developing in childhood or from traumatic events. With fear prohibiting you from expressing your thoughts and emotions in the moment, as a child does, you may turn to diversions or distractions, hoping to ignore and repress what causes you the most harm. A reliance on work, romantic or sexual partners, drugs, alcohol, social media, or other escape methods all scream, "Help! I have a problem weighing on me, but I can't let it out!" Or you may be more guarded than ever, never letting anyone in to see the emotional part of you that desperately needs attention, and eventually, all that fear in you will rot and turn into anger or anxiety.[1] But what happens when you bottle your emotions and then experience an event that puts you over the edge? The same thing that happens when you throw compressed air into a fire. Boom!

In the animal world, if you're rejected, you die. You need a pack or tribe to stay protected and fed. If you express yourself in an unsafe environment, where you experience rejection (for whatever reason, many having nothing to do with you), your primal survival instincts kick in, and you will hide aspects and attributes to fit in. Fear takes over and your confidence in who *you* are diminishes. You are most likely accessing the *external* opinions, biases, and perspectives of your surroundings (or community). When you feel strongly that there's a disconnect between your real emotions and the external opinions, imposter syndrome sets in, increasing your anxiety and making you feel like "a fraud." You don't "air your dirty laundry," and instead, you suppress and oppress who you really are. You lose faith in yourself when you do not *practice* faith in yourself.

That's why you need the air element: to put space between yourself and your emotions so you can air it out, adopt a third-person perspective on your own feelings, and bring objectivity into the equation. That way, you can both validate yourself and find your way past it.

The air element is associated with the fifth chakra, known as *Vishuddha* in Sanskrit. The chakra resides in your throat, a bridge between your heart and mind that allows you to bring forth the emotions deep within and express them out loud. Whereas the wood element centers around shrugging off the "should"s from your shoulders, air focuses on expression. You don't just "let things go" when you practice air—you scream and cry and laugh and sing your heart out, letting heaviness float out of your body, through your throat, and into the air around you. It is release in its purest form—particularly, releasing fear, the root of all negative emotions.

Too little air in your life can result in a "heavy heart, heavy soul." People may start telling you to "lighten up," "just smile," or "see the silver lining," but when you're in the thick of emotions, too tangled up to even understand what you're feeling, just talking won't do you any good. Your feelings have you in a chokehold, applying pressure and forming that lump in your throat that you can't swallow. Eventually, it becomes so enveloping that it takes over your life, distracting you from anything else. You see your life through the shroud of pain and disappointment and walk around like Eeyore from *Winnie-the-Pooh*.

Air empowers you to insert space between you and your emotions.

The way to create this separation is through expression, decompressing your emotions that were oppressed in your system to let the pressure off, release some of the intensity, and be able to step back to look at them from afar. Swallowing your tears, anger, or emotions will simply push them deeper, eventually depositing them in a body space where you think you can hide them. It may be easier to "just cry about it," but to actually immerse yourself in the feelings as they pour from your body and stay non-judgemental is much harder.

When faced with truly daunting situations, humans naturally feel overwhelmed and unable to process emotions because they don't feel safe. Like the little Dutch boy who holds back an entire river of water by plugging a hole with his finger in a dyke, most fear that if *they* unplug their finger from their own defense mechanisms blocking their emotions, their whole facade will collapse and these emotions will come flooding out. Trying to stop a perceived tsunami is inconceivable, and most fear that once these emotions gush fully out for everyone to see, they will not be able to pick up the pieces and they will be rejected, saying, "If you knew me, you wouldn't like me." They don't want to have an eternity of brokenness—they do not know what is on the other side of this full excision. And the unknown is scary.

Even when you're in an unsafe environment, there is a way to create a safe bubble within it, to make space for honest communication, to let some air in. To take in air is to take in life and everything it has to offer. Lungs are your best detoxifying filter system. Why do you think "just breathe" is such a common adage? When you inhale, you bring attention to the tightness and restriction that's holding you back; when you exhale, you let it all go and make way for your voice to come through, loud and clear.

Think of your mouth and throat as the instrument through which the air in your lungs creates your voice. Your head provides the accumulated data and your heart tempers and shapes your wording. Here is a suggestion of how to create a safe space to articulate a "touchy" subject. First, take some needed space before speaking about what you're feeling. Then, ask for permission to vocalize your thoughts, feelings, and opinions. This preps the other person for it and gives them a chance to let you know if they will listen or not. *What* you say is one thing, but *how* you say it is quite another. Here is an example my father used for years. Hear the difference between angrily calling someone a "son of a bitch" and calling someone a "*creative* son of a bitch." The *what* you say comes from your brain's assembled experience and knowledge, and the heart is *how* you say it.

Preparation is key.

While I'm all for expressing yourself with authenticity, there is an *acceptable* way and an *unacceptable* way to go about it. If you make the receiver of your communication the target of your anger and pain, you make your problem someone else's problem, giving their actions power over your feelings. This is an important point. You're no longer expressing—you're projecting, putting your receiver on the defensive. In other words, you will not be heard.

There's another clearly "wrong" method of expressing, and that's when you resort to violence—against others or yourself. Aggressive behavior only leads to more physical, emotional, and psychological destruction and gives the receiver a battle to join, something to defend against, making a mess out of your emotions instead of clearing them up for you.

If you yell at the person you love just so you can be heard, you're projecting your voice into a negative void that will only reflect back at you when they yell in defense. No one is ultimately being heard. By instead saying, "Let's have an open discussion," you can create separation for yourself, not just *within* yourself but also *between* you and the other person, so they can receive what you're experiencing instead of putting their guard up.

Sometimes, you can't express your emotions to another person. When you're angry, for example, even being in the presence of another person could make you so mad that you can only see red. I don't believe you can reason with all your emotions. Emotions as heavy as anger or sadness cannot only be talked about—they demand to be expressed. Straight and simple.

If you let deep, unsettling fear sit in the pits of your stomach, it simply grows and grows, and before you know it, it is ugly—a disease—and leads you down a path of regrets. Many of these emotions feel like regret, guilt, and shame. Instead, acknowledge your fear by expressing it. Say what you're feeling, cry about it, scream about it. Let it out and stare at it. When it leaves your system, you've created space between you and the emotion. Now, you can actually see it for what it is and move past it. To quote Louise Hay, "If we are willing to do the mental work, almost anything can be healed."[2]

Air: Questions to Ask Yourself

- Am I being truthful with myself?
- Am I speaking my truth to others?
- What am I not expressing?
- Where am I oppressed?

EXPRESS, DON'T REPRESS

During one of my travels, I visited Nrityagram, an out-of-the-way "dance village" in South India. Nrityagram is India's first modern-day Gurukul, or residential school, where the community learns traditional, extremely technical Indian dances from a young age.[3] The first time I witnessed these young women dance, I felt an immediate connection. Every move was curated. With a single flick of the finger or bat of an eyelash, the symbolisms accumulated into a soul-touching narrative. Every movement signified meaning and had an intention behind it. In the words of the founder, Protima Gauri:

> I [dreamed] of building a community of dancers in a forsaken place amidst nature. A place where nothing exists, except dance. A place where you breathe, eat, sleep, dream, talk, imagine—dance. A place where all the five senses can be refined to perfection. A place where dancers drop negative qualities such as jealousy, small-mindedness, greed, and malice to embrace their colleagues as sisters and support each other in their journey toward becoming dancers of merit. A place called Nrityagram.[4]

After watching them practice, I had the opportunity to eat a meal and chat with the women. They told me more about their art and culture, which vividly reminded me of West African dance and its intricacies. One wrong move while dancing, and they'd portray a completely different message from what they intended. In this particular performance, without the words of Shakespeare or Chaucer, the dancers were able to depict a narrative, a tale as old as humanity: a barren, young maiden would not have children and therefore would never marry, destined to spend her life alone.

Enlightened by the experience, I returned to my hut near Bengaluru, complete with a wood-stocked fireplace and thatched roof, where I was staying with my boyfriend. Southern Indian superstition says that a snake crossing your path denotes a bad omen, particularly deception. And while no snakes crossed our paths during the day, one did slither its way into our bed one night.

The superstition held true. During our last day in India, my boyfriend confessed, "I want our relationship to go back to the way it was before we committed to each other." Turned out, he was an open-relationship kind of guy. I was heartbroken. We had journeyed together all over Japan, China, and India, and now, all of a sudden, we were over.

Our last moments together were like a sad rom-com with no happy ending. He dropped me off at the airport, I turned around and said goodbye, and as soon as I turned back to board the plane, I just couldn't hold it in any longer. I broke down. The tears would not stop, and I didn't want them to. I kept telling myself it was all okay, just let it all out. And I did . . . for nine straight hours until I reached the US. I made a commitment to myself that once the wheels of the plane touched down on the JFK tarmac, I would not shed a tear about him any longer—and I didn't. By the time I landed, I felt drained, having squeezed the emotions out of my body like a sponge. I let myself feel all of it: the hurt, the betrayal, the pain, the anger, the sadness. Having expressed myself to the fullest extent, I didn't cry or scream about him ever again. Not one drop of grief was left.

I put air and space between my emotions and myself. I felt the emotions from the very depth of my being, pushed them all out, and released them into the air. And because of that, I was now light enough to float.

CLEAR YOUR THROAT

Expression isn't needed only for "big deal" emotions. Sometimes, the little things in life may frustrate you the most. If you don't express these little frustrations, setbacks, or annoyances, the sorrow and agony build up until you explode. Let me give you an example.

Just the other day, I let out a blood-curdling scream. No one was trying to murder me nor had I hurt myself—I was simply trying to insert my mattress into a fitted sheet. Now, I'm sure you agree that fitted sheets are the worst part of making your bed. But that's not the sole reason I had a mini-explosion. Let me back up a bit and tell you the events leading up to this.

I woke up that morning with a stomach ache. I was in the middle of my annual detox and was naturally drained. My body begged me to take a nap, but I knew I had to do my chores. So, I pushed my body to do laundry instead of listening to it.

You may have already made the connection by now, but let me explain anyway. A friend was helping me make the bed and became confused when I barked out a directive. Her defense mechanism kicked in, and suddenly, I lost my cool—I screamed so loud it stilled the very air in the room.

A few seconds later, after we each took in a breath, we finished making the bed. But we were both shocked by how the situation escalated in a matter of seconds. Why had I just burst out like that?

> ### Symptoms of Disconnect with Air
>
> - Feeling a lump in your throat or overwhelming emotions
> - Difficulty in breathing or tightness in the lungs
> - Desire to smoke tobacco and cannabis (to suppress grief situated in the lungs)
> - Cough and a build-up of phlegm
> - Chronic lung and throat issues
> - Low, resigned voice (like Eeyore)
> - Feeling physically "deflated" or emotionally "lifeless"
> - Feeling helpless, restricted, or incarcerated as if you have no control over your own life
> - Reacting defensively to most situations

The next day, when catching up with another friend, I told him about the incident, and he told me what he thought: "You just needed to let it be known that you were feeling an unrest, an irritation, and you simply were not going to let it be glossed over."

Now, I realize how true that assessment was. Clearly, my body wanted one thing and my mind wanted another: my body pleaded with me for rest, and I kept pushing and pushing until finally it just couldn't take it anymore. My body let out its frustration through a scream, wanting my mind to pay attention, give it a break, and address its needs.

Remember when I said the throat connected mind and heart? The scream was literally a cry for help, a cry to stop pushing, pushing, pushing, and to self-nurture instead.

After I opened my throat and yelled, I did feel lighter, and I did end up doing some self-care. But what would've happened if I never expressed discomfort? I probably would have pushed my body even more, caused it to completely break down, and likely blown up in the face of my friend in the process. Instead, by releasing the deep unrest, I delivered a wake-up call to myself.

I needed attention.

I needed to be cared for.

I needed to take a breath and let in air.

When I did, everything changed for the better.

Here's what happened without me even realizing it: I cleared my throat of all obstruction without holding back. I'm sure you've experienced a lump in your throat before, where you feel like you just can't swallow it even as you slowly choke. Since I couldn't keep trying to swallow, I instead spit "the frog in my throat" out in the form of a scream. For me, the lump was exhaustion, but it could result from any emotion: fear, stress, guilt, shame, anger. Constriction in any form signifies that you're holding back. Suppressing. But if there's no openness in your airway, you won't be able to take in breath—*prana*, or "life"—which explains why you won't be able to just ignore it. If there's a lump, it's because you're trying to swallow something that is painful or emotional. Push it out instead! Throw a tantrum, starting from your feet all the way up your body and out of your mouth, like a volcano that builds pressure until it finally explodes. I was a pent-up volcano, and the scream was my release.

What's yours, and when is it coming?

Emotional Clarity Exercise

Partner up with someone, and ask them to place one hand on your upper back, against the fourth chakra (your heart), and another hand on your mid-back, near the third chakra (your solar plexus). Start speaking. Talk about something that is weighing on your mind, and feel the vibrations where your partner has placed their hands. Feel and hear the difference in your voice when your emotions emerge from these areas that are supported.

Now that you know what this feels like, try to replicate these feelings the next time you try to communicate your feelings to someone else. Reflect on how calm the feeling makes you, how it prepares you to first create a safe space, and then calmly express your thoughts and emotions.

Project your voice without straining it.

Direct all the energy from deep in your body, all the way up and out, and not just from your throat.

Feel the sound of your voice and emotions through your entire body, like air rushing through you.

By grounding yourself this way, you can prevent yourself from expressing the *wrong* way. You won't spiral into spewing hate onto someone else or violently attacking them. Instead, you'll be able to be objective, express it all out into the air, and take it from there.

Release can occur in different forms, not just your voice. Let me give you another example. I once modeled for a painter who lived out in the country. At the time, I was still going through my divorce, and I found out that my soon-to-be ex-husband did something to really upset my boys. I was furious. I felt absolutely *wild* with anger. That night, we built a big country bonfire, and I helped everyone gather sticks and trash to throw in—I was literally fueling the fire both outside and inside me. While foraging for more wood, I found a machete in the barn.

With this primal destructive implement in hand, I expressed my anger and frustration to a point that even surprised me. I lost myself in a fire dance, and when I came across a clearing with big, thick patches of pampas grass, I cut them down, hacking away at their bases as if each stem connected directly to my ex-husband. I chopped at the illusion, slashing away all the dead emotions and still-lingering ties that bound me to him. After a while, the rage subsided, and I left behind piles of dead grass. I had literally "cut through the chaff." As I looked down, I noticed my bloody hands, ripped open by the extreme effort I put in.

There was no way I could've talked about these feelings and felt the same release. By huffing and puffing with exertion as I hacked and hacked, the symbolism was profound. When I finished, no negativity existed within me anymore or took up vital space; it flew out into the open air, and I could breathe again.

DO YOU WANT MY OPINION?

Practicing release and expression brings great change in you. It builds your confidence muscle and creates an internal calmness of a strong and realized spirit. Those around you can feel it. They can sense the separation you've accomplished between yourself and the emotional weight most people carry. And when they recognize that, they'll come to you for advice and to express their own feelings. Believe me, if I had a nickel for every time someone has called and vented to me . . .

Here are a few tips to make space for others to express themselves and support their self-discovery. First, as soon as someone calls or shows up asking if they can "talk to you about something," your first question has to be, "Do you want to just spew, or do you want my help?" Some people simply need the space to vent their emotions—which is fine, as long as they don't push their toxic burden onto you. However, most of the time, they will want your help. When you start off by defining those expectations for them and yourself, they will be much more prepared to receive your insight. Again, it's all about preparation.

If they say yes, they want your help, then you need to make sure they tell you *everything*. Get it all out of their system. There shouldn't be a single drop of the negative juju left within them. Let them air it all out—no dirty laundry should be left in the bottom of the laundry basket; make room for some air in there!

After everything is out in the open and they're drained from all the stories and complaints they've expressed, they will finally start to breathe. Allow them to take in air and see the emotions they let out. Then, ask for permission one more time: "Do you want my opinion?"

A longtime friend of mine moved to Portland from Knoxville, Tennessee. When he lived in the ultra-conservative Southeast region of Knoxville, he never felt free enough (or accepted enough) to express himself fully. In Portland, he easily found a community more like him. He began surrounding himself with like-minded and like-hearted people. His heart felt less restricted, and despite his initial fear, he ventured out and expressed his true inner being. During a phone call, he told me that opening up his heart was so painful that it felt like lightning was striking it.

When he vented a bit more, I asked him, "Do you want to know what I think?" He said yes, so I continued. "Do you remember what it feels like when your leg falls asleep? When you finally get some blood circulation in there, don't you feel that painful tingling of pins and needles? There are parts of your heart that have been numb for so long that now, as it wakes up, the energy centers are opening up, and it hurts. The circulation is back, the flow of energy is pushing past the blocked and stale parts, and therefore, the pain you feel is just your heart beginning to open up again."

When he heard that, he felt incredible peace. He received what I told him because I asked for permission first, but more importantly, he finally understood. The pain did not indicate something larger about himself, that he was incapable of love or change. No, the pain he felt was just making way to receive love and pleasure later.

Air Affirmations

- I am the messenger.
- I am needed.
- My gifts are destined.
- I am unique and deserve expression.
- To not express what I truly feel or can do is hiding my God-given gifts from everyone.

FINDING MY VOICE

When I was emailing an old friend whom I hadn't seen in over 10 years, he shared a memory that I had forgotten.

He wrote: *"Remember the night we went to Leanne's house and I sang that Hebrew song? It was a peak experience for me. Sometime later, we tried to sing in the car together, and you couldn't. You told me that you did not feel safe singing around me because you didn't feel good enough. Remember any of that? I was sad that you did not feel safe to sing in front of or with me. I think we tried harmonizing 'Amazing Grace.'"*

It's funny that my name is Angel, derived from the Greek word meaning "messenger from God," because I have always loved to sing—just not in front of anyone.

Years ago, while talking to my sons, I remembered how I used to sing my favorite songs while taking them to school in the mornings. One of my sons, who is a musician now, rolled his eyes and said, "Yeah, Mom, and we know every word to every song of Alanis Morissette and *Rent*!" He then proceeded to recite all the words to "Bitter Little Pill" and the *Rent* song, "Seasons of Love." Scoffing a little, he even claimed they were "prisoners" of my off-key singing during those morning car rides! Was I *that* bad?!

Well, I decided, *it's time to change that!*

I looked for a voice teacher and started taking lessons. It was a kick in the ol' internal confidence, but my voice teacher approached me with understanding and firmness. She trained me using somatic terminology, so I could grasp these new concepts. About 18 months went by, and I was sure I was a frustrating student with my inconsistent commitment to my lessons and homework. During the same time, I received a harmonium, also called a "reed organ," as a gift and attended the Kirtan Leader Institute to train with Mike Cohen, master trainer.[5] This is where I learned to play and lead a *kirtan*, a gathering where participants join in singing mantras or prayers. At the institute, I led a group chant with my loving, understanding fellow students and heard my shaky voice over a microphone for the first time.

A few months later, my voice teacher asked me to perform—to actually lead her church's congregation in a "Jesus chant" with a harmonium accompaniment. Though flattered and in disbelief, I set up a serious practice schedule. Eventually, Sunday arrived, and nervous, I sat down in front of the congregation and spoke of the creation of the music accompanying this mantra and the deeper meaning of the Sanskrit words. A mantra has a call-and-response structure, so I invited the congregation to do something new. After the service, some of the congregation showered me with praise and appreciation, and the minister was genuinely grateful and asked me to come back again. My inner critic didn't think I was all that good, yet his and the congregation's words of praise kicked my critic's butt!

Just a few months later, I was leading the choir in two beautiful hymns and got another big self-esteem boost from a different voice coach who was on the piano that Sunday. She took me aside for a few minutes beforehand to build my courage so I could lead a beautifully trained choir in these hymns. She didn't hear my inner critic and pushed me to command my notes. I believe I was truly better that Sunday and graciously appreciated the praise after the service. I was finding my voice, and it was delightful.

Recently, I received some hands-on energy work with a healer who was connecting heaven and earth through my throat area and clearing all the blocks there. During this, I had a vision of my guides and ancestors looking down at me with adoration like a baby. I began to chuckle uncontrollably while, simultaneously, tears rolled down my face. Then, the face of a close spiritual friend appeared in the vision. She bent close and opened her mouth as if to teach me to match my highest vibration with my voice. I started to laugh and cry tears of joy. Part of my prior hesitation to sing had been my deep knowledge that my voice was not matching my higher vibration, so it sounded dysphonic and saddened me when I heard it. But now, I mastered my voice—and how it flowed out of me.

In the spiritual world, the godly or angelic realm is home to the highest vibrations, and evil—feelings such as guilt, shame, or violence—create the lowest vibrations. These vibrations influence you and your actions, and sometimes, you can even *feel* it taking hold of you. You need to always aim to raise to your highest vibration so it can knock out all the debris caught in the lower vibrations of your body and psyche.

According to my name, I was sent as a messenger with a message from heaven, yet I had been diminishing the delivery and "dumbing down" the words and vibration to fit in and be understood. Who am I to judge what those around me will understand? By not speaking and singing from my highest vibration, I had been robbing the listener of its intended message. My intent now is to "tap into the higher vibration," receive its message, and trust myself to deliver it wholly, and those who hear it in their own way will hear the message meant for them. I've become the messenger I was always meant to be.

Finding my voice also taught me another lesson: the air element does not only encourage the expression of negative emotions, such as anger, fear, and sadness. The expression of *all* emotions is required for balance. And, perhaps surprisingly, a significant emotion that many people suppress is *joy*.

Some may be afraid to express joy because the society around them has created a culture where expressing happiness is not normal.

"If they think I'm too happy, they'll hate me."

"I don't want to express my joy because that will make them jealous."

"If I laugh out loud, they'll think I'm being obnoxious and gossip, 'What are they so happy about?'"

Here's what I say: forget them! Don't be like the average commuter on the tube in England with their noses buried in a paper, not even glancing at the people around them, let alone connecting or sharing a smile.

Be happy.

Laugh until your belly hurts.

Roll down a hill.

Do what gives you joy and show it! This will spread—it's contagious in the most beautiful way!

Express everything you're feeling—positive emotions, negative emotions, and everything else in between. Everyone has a voice and a reason to be "here." Don't let others dictate what you say or don't say. Air it all out. *Breathe in. Breathe out.*

Align with Air

Here are some resources that will help you align with the air element within you and beyond you.

Air Spotify Playlist:

Move with Me Videos:

FOCUS ON METAL

METAL	Straight, deliberate, intentional	Refine your **goals**.	Strengthen commitment.	Self-discipline
6th Chakra:				
Third eye		**Direct** yourself toward your needs undistracted.	Find your dedication. Fine-tune your focus.	

Over the years, I have done my fair share of manifesting—the practice of visualizing what you want in life so it can transpire into reality. However, a simple mental image of your goal will not convince the universe to magically make it happen. The visualization process may help you define a direction to follow, but bringing a dream to fruition requires discernment, dedication, and commitment. In other words, intentional discipline.

The Latin root word in "manifest," *manus*, means to bring joy to your life with your own hands—not envisioning a dream, releasing it into the universe, and thinking, *Poof, it's out of my hands now*! Sure, pinning your hopes on fate may come easy, but I do not prescribe to inaction, especially since one of the elements I have taken such special care to hone—metal—advocates for the opposite mentality.

When you practice metal, if you want something to happen, you need to *do* it yourself, for yourself. Ambitions do not materialize if you hide in a closet and wish them into existence. Instead, like attracts like. By taking intentional action on your end, you can attract the same energy and opportunity from the universe around you. The act of manifestation places your dreams in the fifth dimension, outside the realm of reality. For those goals to reach actualization in the real world, the third dimension, human interference is required. So, if you wish to accomplish your fantasies here on Earth, funnel your infinite dreams into finite resolutions.

Metal: Questions to Ask Yourself

- What are my goals?
- How am I distracted? What is my remedy?
- What is my "why"?
- Why do I lack focus?
- How do I feel whenever I make progress?
- Why do I let people or situations stand in my way?
- What am I committed to?
- How will I support my determination?

The sixth chakra, the third eye, empowers you to stick to resolutions, work with a purpose, and focus without being distracted by every new shiny object, person, or opportunity. Referred to as *Ajna* in Sanskrit, the third eye is located in the center of your forehead, just above the eyebrows, and is the seat of direct spiritual vision, intuitive knowledge, self-mastery, and wisdom. It is believed to hold the key to universal knowledge and helps you determine the right path, objectives, and choices in the quest of life.

Hinduism posits the belief that the human mind contains the accumulated experiences of the soul, not only from the beginning of your life in the womb but also throughout each of your past lives. Rooted in the concept of reincarnation, the third eye is likened to a library that contains records of every event witnessed in each life, meaning it influences your opinions, perspectives, and biases in the present day. This is also known as the Akashic Records, essentially a spiritual and metaphysical library that exists as an integral part of our universe, an accumulation of all that has transpired since the very beginning of creation.[1] By climbing to the "highest" perspective (i.e., unlocking your third eye), you zoom out your vision, gain access to the Akashic Records, and see a 30,000-foot view of your "why." Why do you want to achieve your goal? Why do you hold this achievement in high regard? How are you personally invested in the end result? Pair your discernment with the metal element, and you become an unstoppable force of pure energy, making better choices and rocketing toward your goals.

Self-Reflection Exercise

Like with all elements, metal starts with your breath. To reach discernment, you must first distance yourself from the chaos of human life. Turn everything off—your phone, the TV, the lights—and shut the door. Let everything around you become quiet so all you can hear is the faint sound of your own breathing. Check your distractions at the door, whether they be work stress, relationship issues, or health problems. From here on out, all you should focus on is allowing a higher plane of existence from where you can see and sense *everything*. This is the best time to let in the loftiest of thoughts, those that may even seem unattainable, into your vision.

What are your relationship, health, career, or family goals?

What's your "why" for each?

What has worked in the past?

What hasn't? (These are your distractions and course destroyers.)

Walk back from these goals and set attainable benchmarks—steps that get you closer to your goals. Write all this down and set up reminders of the benchmarks on your calendar. Celebrate each accomplishment toward your goals, no matter how small. The movement is forward and onward!

Metal movement is linear, not lyrical. In air and water, you flow, moving as smooth and effortlessly as a stream or a warm summer breeze. But when you practice the metal element, your movements are intentional and straight, similar to marching with discipline. The metal element is a decisive element, usually piercing and straight like a sword that will cut through the chaos and guide you, undistracted, toward your dreams.

However, like most people, you might have moments of uncertainty where you do not know which step to take next. Or you might have conflicting desires that compete for your time—in which case, how do you decide which one deserves more energy? The metal element is about committing yourself to a task and unwaveringly working to accomplish it. Learning to prioritize, though, is a prerequisite for commitment, and like most important skills, it requires practice and dedication.

I have a client who struggles with committing to a plan. She might make a loose, wishy-washy suggestion to meet for lunch with someone but never says, "I'll be there for sure," because what if a better invitation comes along? She may not even realize it, but for her friends who are trying to plan events, her indecisive nature can be aggravating to deal with. At the worst of times, it even feels disrespectful. Though she never verbalizes this, her actions suggest she thinks she will have a better time around other people—in which case, why even make a half-hearted commitment?

I believe that your commitments should either be 100 percent or zero, nothing in between. Pick a path and stick to it. If you make half-assed commitments to anything—people, relationships, careers, or personal resolutions—you receive half-assed results in return. Sure, something better, bigger, and brighter may come your way, but if you want to stay on course to reach your goal, you need to make sacrifices. With metal, sacrifice is a given. To see results, all the whimsical, abstract thoughts and priorities must be exchanged for concrete actions. The way forward is linear, with you on one end and your goal on the other. A straight shot.

The metal element within you will keep you on the straight and narrow—you just need to use it.

Symptoms of Disconnect with Metal

- Indecisiveness and lack of opinions
- Feeling "lost" or directionless
- A negative outlook on life and self
- Fear of commitment
- Easily distracted or the inability to focus
- Foggy brain

YOU NEED A CARROT

When a client comes to me feeling lost or directionless, I always ask them, "What's your why?"

You could have the best daily routine in the world—you wake up early, work out, eat a healthy breakfast, set aside eight hours for productive work time, go to bed early enough so you have eight hours of undisturbed sleep—but your routine means nothing if you don't have a certain "thing" you're working to achieve. In essence, you need a carrot.

Without a carrot, i.e., an intention or purpose at the end of the finish line, you could have textbook discipline and still feel unfulfilled and lost. You need something to work for, a vision that demands your commitment, something your metal element can tune into. Otherwise, what's it all for?

The carrot dangling in front of you can be your target or a reward you dedicate your entire being into achieving. Think Psychology 101. What can act as an intrinsic or extrinsic motivator to help you cross the finish line?

Your carrot doesn't have to be a lofty ambition like "being the president of the United States" or "being the first person to set foot on Mars." (Although, if these *are* your ambitions, go for it!) You can set a simple aspiration, such as working out every day or losing a set amount of weight before a vacation. With the reward of a well-toned body in your mind's eye, you can hone your metal element to support your intentional discipline and commitment to a workout regimen that will actually produce results, rather than giving up after yet another futile and frustrating attempt.

Discipline conjures images of exercise, weight loss, or painful deprivation and sacrifice. However, metal applies to any subject where you need control over your own choices. For example, think about relationships. Do you have a friend who refuses to commit to one person? They always keep the backdoor open, "just in case." But "just in case" of what? Without a "why," they cannot focus the metal element inside them and dedicate themselves to one person—or multiple people, a separate person, or no people at all, whatever they truly desire! They need to ask themselves what they want first. Is their "why," their carrot, to find someone they can spend the rest of their life with? Is it to find stability? Is it to find a person they can wholly connect with? Is it a tall man with blond hair and blue eyes? Is it a beautiful girl who walks with so much confidence that she turns heads? *What's the "why"*? Once they ask themselves specific questions and figure out who they're looking for and what type of relationship, your friend will have an easier time committing. It's about finding direction.

When you're directionless and running in circles, you may feel bogged down by all the responsibilities thrust on you. You can't grasp the motivation to make the best of an opportunity. In fact, you may not even find it in you to give 100 percent of yourself to a goal because your attention is divided between five *other* opportunities! Multiple distractions may cause you to spiral. Remember, opportunities don't mean anything if you can't actually do something to achieve them. Ask yourself, "Why should I pursue the opportunity?" If it pushes you closer to the carrot you want in life—whether the target is money, fame, giving back, publishing a book, building a family, or whatever else your ultimate goal might be—then it's worth chasing. Use your "why" to pull yourself out of the quagmire and the murkiness. Instead of saying yes to every opportunity that comes your way, learn to assess, separate the meaningful ones from the chaff, and say no to those that will simply take away focus that's better spent on a different task. Metal can be your best friend, but only if you practice the word *no*.

Each day brings a new list of responsibilities: your laundry, the dishes, your job, maybe your kids or your partner, your side hustle, your appointments to meet with someone, and then, finally, comes your dream. You may be telling yourself one of these tasks is the "gateway" to accomplishing your dream—"My job will give me the cash flow to pursue my dream years from now!"—but there comes a time when that divided commitment is no longer enough. You're mistaken if you think you can effectively multitask and juggle 20 different obligations when the reality is that you are diluting your efforts in the process. Bring forth your metal: refocus on the one task that's most important to your vision, take steps toward it, and commit to it until it is complete. Then, every time you achieve something toward your goal, give yourself a pat on the back, a reward—buy ice cream, take a cheat day, go see that movie you've been waiting for. Progress begins once you commit to yourself. You owe it to yourself to make your dreams come true.

"A Day in the Life" Meditation Exercise

"A Day in the Life" is one of my most-used active meditations that I guide my clients through, especially when they are in desperate need of some metal in their lives. I ask them to gently close their eyes and quiet their internal distractions. Then, I slowly ask them reflection questions about what their life may look like five years from now:

- As you wake up in the morning, what does your bed feel like?

- Look out of the window in your room. What do you see outside? Where are you living?

- Take stock of your body. How does it feel?
- What do you do next?
- What do you have on your agenda for the day?
- Who do you meet and talk to?
- How do you end your day?
- What have you achieved? What are you still working on?

With every question, I guide my clients to dig in deep and be specific. Five years from now, one of them might look out their window and see downtown New York while others might see a forest. They may take stock of their body and feel physically fit, energetic, their ideal body weight. Their plans for the day might include meeting with the CEO of a company that they've always wanted to partner with or going on a date with someone who looks like their dream version of a partner. They might end their day feeling satisfied and grateful, maybe sharing a glass of wine with a loved one. Visioning is powerful. This is the time to let your imagination go wild with no restrictions or attention to roadblocks. What influences your dream the most are your emotions. In this exercise, allow the smells, tastes, visuals, and feelings to get specific and intense. They are the lighthouses for your visions, beckoning your dreams into reality.

The situations vary for each person, of course, but they all have one similarity: what they imagine five years from now is their "why." Whether they knew about it before the meditation or not, what they visualized was their reason for waking up every morning. Once the meditation clarifies your world for you, your direction and immediate next steps become apparent. Channel the metal element—feel the determination and focus direct you.

Set your eyes on the horizon, and start your journey.

PUT ON YOUR BLINDERS

When I do the "A Day in the Life" meditation exercise, here's what I see: *I wake up feeling my best and I'm off to the races. I have a big day ahead of me. I've got my power suit on, and I'm conducting meetings with important people—I'm talking to them about my screenplays and eating good food. I'm in Hollywood, and my very own TV series is set to launch.*

I've seen the possibilities of what could happen, but to turn my dreams into reality, I need to retrace my steps to the present and consider what I need to do. If I'm to have important discussions with important people, I should probably start working on my screenplays more diligently. Then, I need to broaden my network and put myself out there, and I need to pitch, pitch, pitch my screenplay to the right producers. While the process has not been an easy road, each day I work toward it. I make connections, refine my scripts, and work on my pitch. Slowly but surely, I make progress.

Twelve years before I started writing *Issues in My Tissues*, I put pen to paper and drafted a personal memoir: *The URBhana Way.* I worked on it diligently and bared my heart and soul as I recounted painful stories and the self-discoveries I experienced. I wrote about half of the book when, suddenly, I lost speed. I lost my metal element. As I discovered, you can be aware of what it takes, you can have your "why," and you can be well on your way, but if you let your metal element rust, all is lost. I wrote so much of myself in those pages, but I was never able to bring the book to fruition—until now.

As I write this book, the metal in me is polished and shining. I'm at my most focused, committed, very best self, and I'm invested in putting my story out there—and hell-bent on finishing and publishing it. My "why" now is to help people integrate their minds and bodies, a goal bigger than myself. This is my carrot. And I cannot stop now.

If you knew the former me, you would know that I was the definition of a "distracted diva." Shiny objects get my attention. I'm a fast-flowing rapid, and nothing has ever stopped me. But I've worked hard to attain a quiet, peaceful mind at the moment, all for the purpose of writing my story. I am in a calm and swirling eddy, and my book is rising out of me. On the shoreline, I can see so many shiny opportunities and distractions that are tempting to dissuade my attention, but I keep bringing my metal forth and holding myself accountable to be intentionally disciplined. I have my blinders on and will look nowhere but ahead, where my bookshelf gains a new addition. This time, one with my name on it.

Diane Smith's Story: Committing to Art

When I first attended Angel's somatic movement classes, I could barely move. But with each class, I gained both strength and fluidity, thanks to the various elements Angel honed within me. However, the one element I continued to struggle with was also one that I needed most as a painter: metal. I should've known—I've never been able to walk in a straight line to save my life. Add to that my creative and artistic nature, and focus flies right out the window.

Practicing with Angel revealed the metal in me. When I embarked on a sobriety journey, it took an enormous amount of commitment. As I watched my friends continue partying and drinking their nights away, I had to make a very tough life choice. As of 2024, I've been sober for 32 years. Sobriety was a lonely journey—but it's also the best choice I've ever made. Here's why: I was *finally* able to get back into my art.

I'm a born artist. But in grade school, some of my teachers often told me a career in art was beyond me. They shut me down completely, and with time, I shut myself down too, despite loving my craft and even winning art contests. By the time I started drinking at 16, art was out of my life for good—that is, until decades later, I checked myself into rehab and went sober. I was having a tough time, but another resident there was an artist as well. She told me to paint with her, and when it was just me and my acrylics, everything felt much simpler. I discovered that painting my emotions was easier than talking about them, and through art, I found a way to be me again.

Angel supported me even further. The tools she provided, in addition to the ChakraMents, tuned my focus. Not to mention, her classes and encouragement were the best antidepressants out there. When I felt depressed, I could hardly pull myself off the couch, let alone hold a paintbrush. But Angel and I spent weeks working on my metal, my commitment, my focus. I was once a drone worker in corporate America—successful, sure, but also unhappy, depressed, and sick. Looking back, I realize that box was always too small for me. Now, I'm living abundantly, thriving by doing what I love doing.

Working my metal is an everyday process, but I've gotten better at it. Today, I'm fully dedicated to my art: I receive commissions, sell my work, paint sculptures for public auctions, and donate pieces to charities and events. Art is now a part of everything I do—and with it, so is metal.

I'm the happiest I've ever been.

GIVE YOUR ALL

In chapter one, I defined choice as the space between stimulus and response. The importance of choice does not become more vital than when concerning the metal element. When you begin building habits that put you closer and closer to your "why," obstacles will block your path. Persistent obstacles sometimes take the form of your friends, parents, teachers, peers, or bosses who constantly tell you, "You'll never be able to achieve anything." Even if you try not to let outside perspectives affect you, negativity, especially in large quantities, is bound to soak into your tissues. You begin to self-sabotage and lose all confidence, and before you know it, you've added another squashed hope to the pile. This is the human condition.

Depressing, isn't it? But what if I told you there's a choice . . . that by intentionally putting space between the stimulus (the nay-sayers) and your response, you can actually preserve your sense of self and keep hacking away at your dream? Say you have a bad habit and no one believes that you can ever change. You can respond by passively agreeing or giving up, or you can make a *choice* to insert some space, practice your metal element, and commit to adjusting your habit for the better.

Say losing weight is one of your resolutions. You can either try to crash-diet—an unhealthy way to go about it as you will likely gain back all the weight immediately after—or you can change your unhealthy eating and exercise habits as part of your lifestyle, not a one-and-done pursuit. Patience and celebrating small successes are required here. While you ultimately decide whether you want to change your behavior or not, ensure intention drives your decisions, not apathy or carelessness.

Take my own obligations, for example. I'm often asked to serve on boards of local organizations. You may be thinking, *That's not a difficult choice at all—it's an honor, so say yes!* Each time someone requests my involvement, of course, I feel honored. However, I'm not one who makes less than a 100-percent commitment. If I'm to serve on a board, I want to be fully and undividedly present. First, I need to budget for my time constraints and how much I already have on my plate, and then I can decide if I have the time and energy to dedicate myself to serving on a board. After all, board positions come with trust and responsibility— organizations I donate my time to deserve nothing but my very best. If I cannot give it my all, I will not do it at all. The metal element gives me the backbone to consider an opportunity and then identify the right choice; sometimes, when saying no seems difficult, that's when doing so is the most necessary.

Metal Affirmations

- I know what I want.
- I can say no to distraction.
- I can stay focused.
- I have my goals in focus.
- I practice intentional discipline.

The metal element is one that I have struggled with. At times, my life was a full-force river, and I felt like I could not control what happened around and to me. But metal is a transformational element. As soon as I practiced intentionality and adopted the principles of self-discipline, restraint, and commitment, my life changed. If you're like me and struggle to stick to one undertaking, let me assure you: you can do it, and when you do, your whole world bursts wide open and everything becomes possible. So, find your carrot (your "why").

Grasp it—there's no better time to start than right now.

Align with Metal

Here are some resources that will help you align with the metal element within you and beyond you.

Metal Spotify Playlist:

Move with Me Videos:

INTEGRATE WITH ETHER

ETHER	Cloud-like, angelic, all-encompassing, moving meditation, gentleness	Bring awareness to the **lightness** of your body.	Integrate the mind, body, and spirit.	Integration
7th Chakra: Crown		Float **cloud-like**.	Connect to your highest self.	
		Allow all emotions and thoughts to **exist at once**.	Radical self-acceptance.	

Alex Grey is a wonderful spiritual artist, author, teacher, and Vajrayana practitioner known for his art collection, Sacred Mirrors. The 21-painting series captures the essence of Nirvana—a complete manifestation of the fifth dimension within and beyond the self.[1]

Grey is a master at depicting both the finite elements of human life—the body with its muscles, eyeballs, brain, and nerves—and the infinite element of pure energy. When you accidentally bump into someone on the street, when your shoulder brushes against theirs, you're making contact.

Physical contact. That's it. You don't fully feel their energy or vibrations. Your interaction ends at the physical.

However, if you're a highly sensitive and intuitive person, you may start to pick up on vibrations whenever you're close to someone. Or maybe you've felt it with a partner, when you feel such loving energy coming off of them that it makes you think, *I need to be close to this person.* The feeling you experience is an instance of you tapping into the energetic realm of that person. But how long did it take you to know them before you could get to this stage? Three years? Three minutes? Some people are gifted with the ability to intuitively tap into others' vibrations within *seconds* of being in their presence, but for those without a natural gift for energy, the ether element can help improve the connection between them and other people while also strengthening their link with the cosmos.

Your third dimension is your physical body, your fourth dimension is the energy field that surrounds you, and the fifth dimension is beyond everything—the universe in all its unknown subtle messages and power. Even if you are sometimes aware of the fourth dimension, the fifth is elusive, requiring a certain awareness and allowance of yourself. After all, when you are able to connect with ether, you can achieve your highest self. This takes mastery over your perceived limitations and expands your mind. The fifth dimension is the upper, angelic realms from which you can download messages even beyond human imagination. You can't see it, but by being open to the cosmos and tuning your senses to listen to it, you'll find peace in losing yourself within the dimension.

The ether element is about allowing all things and yourself to be present at once. It resides in the crown chakra, called *Sahasrara* in Sanskrit, and is associated with consciousness and divine wisdom. The crescendo of all the other elements, ether provides the knowledge to align these ChakraMents within yourself and reach your highest potential. The whole of you—the good, the bad, the ugly—coexists; accepting this without judgment brings you closer to divine love. Ether is all-encompassing and inclusive. The utter integration of mind, body, and spirit.

A completeness.

Ether: Questions to Ask Yourself

- Where do I feel the calmest and most comfortable?
- What would I call my sanctuary or sacred space?
- What does my gentle inner voice sound like?
- Where am I able to breathe and connect with nature?
- Can I quiet my mind, or do I need help?
- Do I believe in a greater universe, a higher power, or an omnipotent and loving energy?
- Do I have radical acceptance of myself?

ZOOM OUT

Earth grounds you, water helps you adapt, wood shrugs off the weight on your shoulders, fire allows you to tap into and direct the passion within yourself, and metal focuses you to achieve your goals. Now, ether gives you peace to reconcile with yourself, practice acceptance so you can acknowledge your strengths and weaknesses, and let joy and sadness be there all at once, embracing each emotion with no judgment. You may feel your anxiety draining, being replaced with a sense of belonging and an understanding of your place in the universe. Without ether, you may experience conflict inside, poking your inner critic and saboteur. Ether helps you make peace with yourself, love parts of yourself, and gracefully let go of the rest. Without this internal peace, you'll be too distracted to even make progress with the six preceding elements.

When I first met Angel, I was a little wary. Hearing her Southern accent reminded me of the discriminatory remarks I had heard time and again when I used to live in the South. I decided to steer clear of her . . . Except, when you're on a trip in Bali with 24 random people, you'll eventually end up talking to all of them. Before long, the universe decided it was time for Angel and I to cross paths, and we found ourselves coincidentally sitting at the same table.

She looked me dead in the eyes and said, "Tell me about yourself."

Somehow, by the end of the night, I had not only told her about myself but also opened up about my fears, my negative experiences in the South, and things I never thought I would freely share with anyone—especially a Southerner!

But Angel isn't just anyone. One conversation made that very clear. She was fully tuned in, accepting, and intuitive, and she soon became one of my dearest friends and remains so, even eight years later. That Bali trip is still so memorable to me *because* of Angel. She's wild and fun and so very authentic that you can't help but ease up and laugh around her. Even though we were completely lost in Bali once, driving in circles in a little Vespa in the middle of a zero-visibility rainstorm, being with Angel made that experience an adventure. We thought it was so funny when we kept missing the exit that we were doubled over in laughter.

She is a force of positivity. Always has been. And the biggest reason why she is so capable of meeting others where they are, of projecting vibrations of trust, of embracing her spontaneity is that she has been able to work through her trauma—the "issues in your tissues" as she likes to call it—and emerge a transformed and grounded individual. While her practice is rooted in somatic movement, mine is all about gaining consciousness of your most suppressed self.

I am a shadow worker, the "shadow" being hidden aspects of ourselves; this is true of everyone. The subconscious drives every thought, behavior, and action. I support individuals on their journeys to self-discovery. We unwind and unravel from our programming, conditioning, and beliefs that are not ours or are no longer serving us. Most people believe that their troubles originate from those around them, that if the situation outside themselves were different, they would "feel" different. But this is an inward journey where we begin to set ourselves free.

We all have the ability to transform ourselves, but it's an "inside-out" process. You can transform yourself by "burning down the house," that is, your emotions and mind, in order to rise from the ashes again and again—transforming yourself.[2]

Through my own harrowing journey and not listening to the messages coming to me, I was continually pummeled by the universe. Blaming my *outside* world for my *inner* world turmoil is being a *victim* and giving power away. I shook my fist at the universe and even gave it the middle finger a few times, asking, "What did I do to deserve all this?"

I saw, felt, and believed that everything was happening *to* me, not *for* me. It was only after years of self-work, self-discovery, going "inward," and learning how energy plays a part in our existence that life got easier for me. I am now able to handle deep triggers with grace and ease compared to the outward negative responses that I always had.

It was Angel's immersion in shadow work that soon opened her up to be a powerful channel. Note that I said Angel is a channel, not a medium. A medium connects you to guides, angels, deities, ascended masters, and ancestors in your life. A channel *embodies* them from the depths of their being.

To do this, you need to connect to the fifth dimension, the universe, on a deep, metaphysical level, something that can only be done after you unwind your shadow. There's the physical body, the mental body, the emotional body, and finally the ethereal body. Most of us readily deal with our physical body and somewhat try to reach our mental and emotional selves, but the ethereal body is elusive. Out of reach. In order to grow, expand, and evolve, we need to surrender—it's how we move into a higher state of consciousness. It's all energy-based; knowing all parts of ourselves gives us power. Power to stand strong in any storm.

Self-discovery is self-love. Looking at our shadow is the deepest form of self-love we can offer ourselves.

Tapping into ether, into the fifth dimension, comes down to one essential practice of transcendence: meditation. Meditation is how you can quiet your mind, check your distractions at the door, and set off on a silent, inner journey within yourself. When you meditate, you experience the vibrations of the universe. You zoom out to the point where all your worries and troubles diminish into tiny specks, and you realize that in the grand scheme of things, what you're facing is smaller than the whole. Your challenges are surmountable. And as your anxiety and worries dissolve, you're left with a lingering sense of peace—a knowledge that no matter what, you have a reason for your existence and you have freedom by practicing choice. "Meditation," by the way, doesn't have to look like sitting in a lotus position (cross-legged) for a long time. It happens in many different forms like riding a horse (or a motorcycle like I do), sitting on a bench along a path, or sitting undistracted at home in your favorite comfy chair.

Many people try meditation once and then say, "Meditation is not for me." Let me assure you: meditation is for *everyone*. In many cases, dismissing it as a helpful practice indicates an unwillingness to stop and feel. And of course, skipping across your fjord of emotions and never sinking into the depths of what you are avoiding may be easier, but for any real change to come, you must train your brain to reconcile with your feelings and stop running from your emotions, experiences, and past. Take a breather because you deserve peace. Open your mind and listen to the universe. You have been running for too long—it's time to come home to yourself.

Symptoms of Disconnect with Ether

- Having a hunched-over posture
- Avoiding eye contact or even physically avoiding people
- Constantly in a state of worry and anxiety
- Experiencing melancholy, grief, or guilt
- Feeling defeated or joyless

I didn't even know what meditation was until I was 34. Soon after my divorce was final and I was struggling with being a single mom, I was searching for a child-care program just so I could have some time to myself, to breathe and conquer this mountain of a life that seemed utterly insurmountable to me at the time. One day, in between errands, I walked past a tiny store run by a hippie couple and was instantly drawn to the incense and sparkling crystals. It felt so peaceful and familiar inside. On the community board, I saw a sign that read, "Little Lights Nursery." Intrigued, I called to get more information. I'm so glad I did because, as a result, I met the woman who changed my life: Suprabha. She was a nun from Columbia, South Carolina, who had packed her bags and set off to a monastery in India. There, she studied under her guru, Shrii Shrii Ánandamúrti, who founded Ananda Marga, a global spiritual service organization.[3]

Suprabha knew all about the situation between me and my ex-husband and about how, when he came to pick up the boys, he would sometimes reek of booze. She perceived my inner turmoil and my fears about the well-being of my children when they were with their alcoholic father. One day, after witnessing a fight between me and my ex-husband, she scooped me up lovingly without judgment, took me inside, and told me, "You need to learn how to meditate."

Suprabha took me under her wing and began teaching me everything from the rituals of meditation to the process of meditation itself, coaching and guiding me through all my distractions. I mean, my mind has always been on a hamster wheel, and at the beginning, I could barely focus on anything for more than 30 seconds! Suprabha's homework for me seemed like an impossible challenge: meditate for 20 minutes a day. By then, I must've had my metal element in order because I rose to the challenge. I knew this exercise would help me obtain peace, even during my most arduous moments. Meditative peace is like a screen door allowing the storm to blow through without breaking the door down.

For a couple of weeks, I really struggled but persevered. The practice of letting go in the moment of inner turmoil again and again brought a pleasurable feeling, faster and faster. Working this mental and emotional "muscle," I developed mastery so I could meditate with ease. And oh my God, the way it made me feel! In those minutes of sublime meditation, I would literally dissolve. My entire body would be one with the celestial realm, and I felt as though my consciousness was just one of the many, many streams of vibrations flowing through the universe.

As I was mastering my meditation practice, I took a holistic studies faculty and staff position at the Omega Institute. Up a flower-lined path was the sanctuary, built to feel like an entirely different world. As I walked across the wooden bridge in my bare feet, looking at the koi pond below me, the visceral peaceful feeling poured over me. I entered the quiet room and sat comfortably on the cushioned floor. The door gently closed behind me, and immediately, all sound cut off as though it were a vault. I closed my eyes and observed the feeling of sitting in this space, and my body slowed down. Everything—the buzz, my heart rate, my thoughts—started to drain away as I chanted a mantra under my breath, drowning out the nagging voices in my mind. My mind calmed down to think and feel absolutely nothing at that moment. It was an achievement I am proud of. All I did was follow my breath as I breathed in and out, in and out, over and over.

I simply disappeared.

When your head is so empty of thoughts that you're floating in nothingness, you begin to receive incredible messages from the universe. Sometimes, you're conscious of them, but most of the time, only after you come out of this trance-like state of meditation can you reflect. The ether element within you will magnetize its messages if you're open and willing, aware and allowing. Meditation is as much of a choice as anything else—except it's one that can be life-altering in ways you could never imagine.

Gratitude Meditation Exercise

Find a quiet peaceful place, whether inside or out. Make sure there will be no interruptions—phone calls, electronic notifications, or external annoyances such as sirens or traffic. Get comfortable. You can either stand or sit for this exercise.

Make sure you are in your body by wiggling your toes and squeezing the muscles in each section of your body like flexing your thighs and then letting them relax. Start with your toes, and do this all the way up to the top of your head. When you get to your face, clench your jaws first and then let them relax. Gently close your eyes partially or all the way. Now, imagine your forehead melting like chocolate streaming down your cheeks and jaw, taking any tension with it. Imagine the top of your head and notice any sensations there. This is where you can connect to the pineal gland residing in the middle of your brain, a mood regulator in concert with the limbic system. There is another gland here in the middle called the amygdala. This is the "gatekeeper" between your primal brain stem and the cerebral cortex, and it is responsible for consequential thinking (in other words, it weighs the costs and benefits of your choices). Your amygdala is important as it allows you to pause, evaluate, and respond to make better decisions. Imagine a golden gate between the top of your head and a brightly lit path upwards to the heavens, the universe. Connect this to your higher self, god, goddess, and your guides, who are here to help you.

Breathe in slowly for four to eight counts and exhale for four to eight counts. Following your breath, shut out the chatter in your brain with a calming mantra—one as simple as "I breathe in love, and I exhale stress and anger."

Repeat this again and again as you open the golden gate at the top of your head and let in the beam of light. Allow it to fill you up and make its way to tiny dark places, crevices that you may not have noticed before. Let it open up the closed and sheltered parts of you and shine its loving light into the shadows present. When we slow down enough, sometimes the negative dark aspect of ourselves (the "shadow") seeps up into our mind. But this is when you have an opportunity to surround your body with love as if it were a crying baby. Embrace this hurt part of you, let it be present without judgment, and shift your attention to someone you love. Feel your joy in the moment.

Ether is about allowing it *all* to exist at the same time. As you feel and observe your emotions, marvel at the complexity and intricacy that make you unique. As scenes and feelings flow in and out of your focus, imagine them as individual threads of different colors weaving the beautiful tapestry of your life. You may hug yourself, or sway gently, or raise your arms and float in a nurturing way. Let this lightness bring levity to all your feelings. Let them rise up like clouds. Just *float*. Imagine yourself suspended in the clouds, in space. Listen . . . this is when you can receive messages that otherwise can't get through the cacophony of life. If there is a nagging thought, put it in a balloon, seal it off, and let it float away until it disappears. Stay here as long as you can.

Before you close out this moment and move on, give yourself gratitude for all of the feelings that have been revealed. Give your body gratitude for slowing down enough to be in suspension. Give your mind love for choosing to give yourself this moment. Finally, thank your heart for all it has endured and how it has communicated with you. Bask in your own gratitude, and then slowly open your eyes and move back into your day.

DMs FROM THE UNIVERSE

You may have not started meditating because you're waiting to visit a sanctuary or local yoga place. You may think, *Meditation requires a sacred space, and I don't have the time to take a trip to the Himalayas at the moment, thanks.*

Yes, meditation does require a sacred space, but sacred just means "special." Your sacred meditation space could be a cozy reading chair or a corner of your bedroom. I converted my office closet into my library and altar. I sit on a thick sheepskin in front of my altar and close the doors behind me to separate me and my sacred space from the outside world and all its distractions. You don't have to travel to a fully equipped, noise-canceling sanctuary on the hills (although that could be an amazing once-in-while experience). If you're practicing every day, know that you can find a sanctuary in your home where you can access the ether element within you simply by standing in front of a window and dancing to ether-inspired music. Just remember to turn off everything, including your phone, so the only messages you're receiving are from the universe.

When giving advice about meditation, I typically encourage going inward to happy, loving thoughts and then releasing them one by one to slow down your thinking, eventually arriving at an empty mind. Simply focus on your breath—in and out, inhaling for four to eight counts, then exhaling for four to eight counts. I have also used short mantras to repeat in my head like "Oṃ maṇi padme hūṃ." The point of meditation is to allow something bigger than you to come through the ether and into your consciousness. Ether is like conduit vapor. You may want to receive messages and wisdom about certain questions—and you will—but it won't be in the way you think. Meditation is not an internal, back-and-forth therapy session. Rather than attempting to think through your problems, you need to feel. Let your emotions and nagging thoughts flow through and out until nothing remains but emptiness.

Fear and anxiety may rise up during meditation. Acknowledge that it is there and follow the source. Eventually, it brings the realization that these negative feelings are brought on by some future visualization that hasn't happened yet. This is the moment to give yourself a hug and comfort yourself as you would a scared child, letting those feelings slip away through the arms of your own loving support. This kind of release will give you a floating, cloud-like feeling, as though you are flying with angels. Sometimes, meditation unearths big, ugly scabs that you have to pick at to see the root of a deep wound, but remember, that scab was created because you couldn't address your issues and emotions at the time of the trauma. In order to begin the healing process, expose the trauma, allow the universe to draw out some of the pain, and allow the toxins and tears to flow freely until you're completely drained. When you're so light that you feel like you have no body, only consciousness, the celestial messages will finally reach you. Feel a hug from the universe, and trust what it tells you.

Ether says that you may hurt now, but in the grand scheme of things, you have an ever-flowing amount of time to *live*—and so much to live for. The world around you is expansive and limitless. If you can exist here, access the wisdom of yourself, the lives before you, and the lives around you, then you can overcome whatever little obstacles block your path.

One of the most important messages you'll receive from the universe is that *you belong*. Humans are uncomfortable with rejection; after all, even cavemen knew that rejection equals death. Now, rejection may not be a matter of life and death—although, it very well could be if it drastically impacts your mental health—but it is also a prominent need for basic emotional health. In Maslow's hierarchy of needs, belonging comes right after physiological and safety needs, demonstrating its importance. However, connecting with ether to the fullest extent enables you to realize that the opinions of people on earth play a minuscule role in your overall purpose. The universe embraces, loves, and accepts you without judgment, no matter the perceptions of others or your own self-image.

MASLOW'S MOTIVATION MODEL

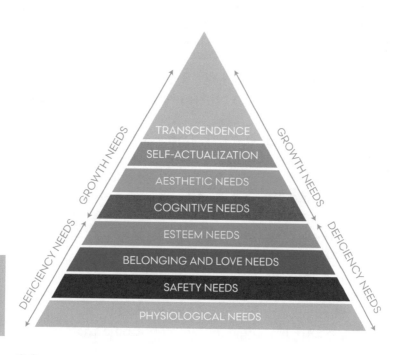

TRANSCENDENCE
SELF-ACTUALIZATION
AESTHETIC NEEDS
COGNITIVE NEEDS
ESTEEM NEEDS
BELONGING AND LOVE NEEDS
SAFETY NEEDS
PHYSIOLOGICAL NEEDS

GROWTH NEEDS

GROWTH NEEDS

DEFICIENCY NEEDS

DEFICIENCY NEEDS

The universe tells you, again and again: *You belong. You belong. You belong. We need you and your gifts.*

Recently, I set off for Arizona on a month-long spiritual trip to a retreat center I had invested in, looking forward to four weeks of meditation, healing, and writing. I drove my car out there with my dogs, my boyfriend, and creature comforts packed for a month. When we arrived at the property, I could only stand there and stare, sucker-punched. The former *ashram*'s demolition and renovations were not on schedule, and somehow, informing me of this had slipped through the cracks. The bunkhouse where I had planned to stay was so terrible it resembled a litter box—literally, since the girl I was sharing the house with never cleaned up after her cat!

Before dropping me off, my boyfriend observed the situation, looked at me, and said, "Oh, honey, you can't stay here." What was I supposed to do? I was embarrassed and deeply disappointed. My dogs and I ended up staying with him in his hotel for the next couple of nights before my "retreat" officially started.

After the shock subsided, I had to face my friends who were responsible for the retreat property oversight. They were my spiritual family. I considered them my tribe. Despite my resolve to try and make it work, I only lasted three days before I had to leave. But in those three days, I meditated on the situation.

The first question I had for myself and the universe was: *How did this happen?* And then, *What role am I playing in this situation, and what is the lesson (sometimes called the "medicine") of this experience?* Not only was I a soul sister with the leaders of this retreat center, but I was also an investor. I had put my faith and money into this and their leadership. I had to look deeper into my motivation to be with this tribe and the past sacrifices I had made just to be a "team player." As I meditated, messages of significant importance began to download. (On a side note, let me point out that if I could meditate amidst chaos, you can find some reasonable space to practice it too!)

The universe urged me to look at my ego. It asked me to reassess my drive to be a part of this tribe and our nine years of friendship together. I noticed an imbalance where taking care of my needs was overshadowed by how much I was surrendering to the needs of others, just to be accepted, loved, and revered. I had sacrificed in order to belong. Of course, compromise and negotiations are a part of all relationships, but I had put everyone else's needs and desires above mine to the point of my own detriment. I saw this pattern in other close and significant relationships around the same time too.

If they held me in the same regard as I held them, would I be sleeping on the floor? Then, realization dawned on me: I didn't have to do this. I should be with people who treat me the way I treat myself, and I would never reduce myself to this level. I would take care of myself with the utmost love, compassion, and respect. As I slowly came out of my meditation, I could see the message crystal clear: *put your needs first.*

So I did. I gently broke the news to the hosts of the retreat, making sure to emphasize that it was to take care of myself, not out of anger with them. (By then, those feelings had already flowed out between us and had given way to healing.) I put all my belongings back in the car, set my cruise control to 90 miles an hour, and set off across the flat Texas desert with my boyfriend and our dogs. We made it back home in 36 hours.

Once I got home, my boyfriend asked me, "What exactly do you want? What are you looking for?" I told him I just wanted some peace and quiet and to be away from everything so I could write or do nothing, to which he replied, "Why not go to our house on the lake? Just throw your keys in the water and turn off your phone when you get there."

As much as I hated admitting it, he was right. I had the most serene place I could think of within my grasp. So, I went there and took care of myself.

When I say meditation can be life-changing, this is what I mean. Who knows what I would've done if I hadn't listened to the universe's message to put myself first? Instead of having a relaxing, productive time, I would've stressed myself out, and who knows how many times down the line I would've allowed people to continue to treat me that way? The ether element within me held my hand and heart through it all and guided me to a much more nourishing place.

Ether Affirmations

- I am connected to my highest purpose.
- I am integrated, and my message transcends.
- I hear the universe's messages.
- I embrace all of me unconditionally.

PEACE, THE MISSING PIECE

In the months leading up to my mother's passing, my cholesterol level was over 300. Three. Hundred. That's how stressed I was. And the only coping mechanism I leaned on was tequila. (This was way before the fire ritual, where I let go of my desire for alcohol.) My mother was 99 years old, and I was doing all I could to make sure she was okay—managing caregivers, delivering all the supplies she needed, sitting by her side, and watching her cling to the life she had left.

I was emotionally fragile and physically exhausted.

The universe gave me a dress rehearsal, however. A few weeks before my mom passed, a dove flew into a nearby window and fell with a thud. I very gently moved the dying dove to a comfortable, safe place hidden in a wood pile. I witnessed that sweet bird's life begin to leave its tiny body. Once the eyes shut, it seemed like its spirit lifted up into the tree above me. I cried uncontrollably. This was the first time I had witnessed death as it was happening. Somehow, it relieved my fear of being there for my mother's death. I told myself again and again, "This dove has prepared me for the death to come. It's teaching me something very important."

I cried my eyes out, but not for long—I had to teach that evening. So I went, and I danced into my grief. As my students and I flowed into the ether movements, soft and cloud-like, I allowed myself to *feel* my grief. Tears streamed down my face. The meditative, dream-like music, the gentle floaty movement of my arms, the sway of my body—I began to feel as though I was finally in a state of mothering myself. I was looking after myself.

The ether movement, which lets you connect with your seventh chakra, your highest self, is all about giving yourself what you need. After seeing death so close, I needed the chance to grieve and prepare for more grief. I danced and danced as tears flowed. I was one with my feelings, which gave me the strength to face the inevitable.

After my mother passed and things settled down a bit, my cholesterol dropped by 100 points, the lowest in 10 years. Let my experience be a testament to how stress affects both the mind and body. The more I practiced the meditative ether element, the more I released myself in its dream-like movements and the more I cherished myself and the world. I was receiving messages that brought me pure bliss.

When you access the divine point of view, you relax. You gain a higher understanding of your experiences and emotions, and you discover the reasons behind who you are and why you are here. *Peace* is the missing *piece* to making sense of your life. Viewing the workings of the world from a zoomed-out perspective empowers you to feel at home within and beyond yourself, leading to salvation. Nirvana.

My favorite way to access the divine is through movement. Ether movements are gentle and cloud-like. Allow everything to be there, take all the elements you played with and learned from, and integrate them into yourself so you can connect to your highest form of being. During these movements, I partially close my eyes and allow the gentle music to lull me into soft motions so I can integrate and let go at the same time—a suspension of the body and mind that lets you float up and up. As you practiced the earth, water, wood, fire, air, and metal elements, a lot of emotions, traumas, and experiences might have come up to the surface, shaken out, entering your awareness. Now, it's time to take all of that and accept it for what it is. Acknowledge that you need to do the work, but also let go of any shame or guilt that might have arisen with it. Working on yourself can be intense. But you're here. You're okay. You will live and conquer and move forward forever. The universe is here and everywhere, right by your side.

You're ether, inside and out.

Here are some resources that will help you align with the ether element within you and beyond you.

Ether Spotify Playlist:

Move with Me Videos:

CHOICE EQUALS FREEDOM

The writing world believes there's a book inside everyone. As I go from having all of these insights, practices, and experiences in my mind to putting it all on paper, I have a sense of birthing something wonderful that will help people from all walks of life. As a somatic movement therapist and confidence coach, I put together the ChakraMental Method™ for the sole purpose of helping my clients get back into their bodies; integrate their physical, mental, and spiritual senses of self; and heal, grow, and move by tapping into the elements within.

Writing this book has brought out the mothering—nourishing and fierce—side of me as I create each word, sentence, paragraph, and chapter to hold immense meaning and act as a resource in your journey of self-discovery and awareness. My fierceness keeps me in check any time I'm distracted, forcing me to keep writing and prioritizing *you*, my reader, above everything else on my task list for the day.

I hope that by reading my stories you've experienced moments of catharsis or even simply an awareness of how the elements play an integral part in your life. If you have found they impact your actions and emotions, then why shouldn't you be more intentional and conscious of them? Why shouldn't you take matters into your own hands and change the way you perceive your body, emotions, and habits? I want you to reach inside yourself, pull out all your good, bad, and ugly stories as I have, and take a look at them from the outside. Writing it all out has put space between me and my experiences. Similarly, writing, dancing, talking to a friend, or meditating can all do the same for you. You just need to find the strength to do it.

I'm a somatic movement therapist first and foremost after all, so my prescription for your health is this: find an empty space in your home or anywhere, put on some music, and *move*. I don't care if you're performing wild acrobatic moves or are just shimmying and swaying on the spot. Do what feels natural. Play the kind of music that resonates with you. Soften your eyes, shut your mouth, and let your body do the talking. I sometimes do this in my kitchen while I prepare a meal. If you've reached the end of the book and still feel self-conscious, then reflect on why. With a solid understanding of the elements, you have learned that the body needs to speak, not just the mind. I imagine that you're way past the point of being the lost person you might have been when you first picked up this book. You are now deeply aware of the elements and chakras within you—so *feel* them. Let them speak. Surrender.

In the beginning, you may need to remind yourself to view life through the lens of elements. *Am I feeling unfocused because I lack metal? Am I having trouble shifting directions because my water element is undernourished? Am I getting angry too easily because my fire element is out of control?* But before you know it, this kind of thinking and recalibration becomes a natural, unconscious part of your behavior, as it has become for me. I don't always need to dig my toes into the earth to feel grounded or go swimming to feel one with the water element. All I need to do is become aware of what I need and use the ChakraMents to shift the way I respond to the issue inside and the world and its triggers outside.

Meditate—it's the gateway to knowing, changing, and healing your inner self. Meditation slows the anxiety and "hamster wheel" in your brain and creates space to reflect and release the intensity of your emotions. The more you practice, the easier it becomes to connect with the ChakraMents. Soon, like me, you'll be able to sit in an airport and easily block off the world around you to meditate for a few minutes.

In addition to meditation, another one of my favorite ways to practice the elements daily is through chakra cards. I pick one out of my deck in the morning, read which chakra is printed on the card, and dedicate my day to it. For example, if a card says "release," then my day will center around the throat chakra. As I carry out my tasks and responsibilities for the day, I stay aware of what's weighing on my shoulders or bringing me down and take a moment to voice it and release it into the air. By focusing on one element at a time, your concentration will help you observe various ticks and sensations in your body, how your mindset shifts over the course of 24 hours, and most importantly, how you can bring both your mind and body together to accomplish everything you want.

While writing this book, I realized that I have *always* lived in my body, and unlike many people, I cannot "escape" it. Some people separate themselves from their bodies during a traumatic event, whether that be jumping out of a plane or getting poked with a needle at the doctor's office. Others fly out of their bodies when in intense, angry screaming matches, flying off the handle and saying words they do not mean when threatened. A ton of people go about every day, barely attuned to their bodies' needs at all and instead in la-la land for the majority of the time! If you find you are one of these people, I urge you to use this book as a reference for your needs. Whenever you encounter a roadblock, insurmountable obstacle, or valley of despair, stop and ask yourself:

- How do I feel?
- Can I name this feeling?
- What do I need?

Then, flip through the pages of this book, identify the element in distress, and address your needs. If you're feeling unmotivated but a deadline is looming closer and closer, flip to the chapter on the metal element and read all about it. If you're feeling out of your depth in a new job, scan through the explanation of the water element and try to go with the flow. This comprehensive book on your inner elements is more than just a collection of insights, exercises, and information—it's a lifeline. Use it as such.

You've come a long way since when you first picked up this book, which means you now have the awareness and the language to identify exactly what's not working for you. The ChakraMental Method™ creates a tangible medium to express the abstract limitlessness within you, putting it into words that can be easily shaped and approached so you can make change happen on your own terms. To name something is to have power over it. When you label your feelings of dissociation as a lack of the earth element, you then know to sit on the ground cross-legged and imagine your spinal cord going deep into the earth and taking root to anchor yourself. Similarly, say you wake up one morning feeling low and think, *Oh God, why am I so depressed*? Maybe your next thought will be, *Ah, I need fire. I need to do something that makes me feel fierce, free, and passionate.*

While the method detailed here uses the elements to describe the body's needs, use whatever vocabulary suits you best. Maybe you feel antisocial one day, as if you will just explode if even one person pokes the bear because you have so much bottled up, waiting to be released. I may label that feeling as a disruption in your air element and encourage you to let those feelings out in a more productive way, but you can label this however you wish. Instead of "air," you could say you feel "prickly," "pokey," or whatever best describes your experience. The elements detailed in the ChakraMental Method™ simply provide a framework to set you free!

Especially if you're in a corporate world that believes in nothing but deadlines and profits, finding your creativity and confidence can be more difficult than usual. See the elements as a tool that gives you an edge—a mastery and control over your emotions, anxiety, and perceptions about the inescapable stresses of society like government, war, money, and so on. You are expected to internalize and process so much grief, stress, and hardship every single day, but remember, what's inside your head is a choice. And *choice equals freedom*.

Allow the elements to be there for you, to give you a space where you can bring in your right to choose, a space to reflect and heal. Take a breath, put a name to what you're feeling, choose how you want to view it and address it, and do what comes naturally to you. When it comes to you, your body, and your mind, no one but *you* has the right to make a decision. Remember to always put the oxygen mask on yourself first before you offer to help anybody else.

In other words, put yourself first. The rest will follow.

As this book comes to a close, I hope you've been able to find the path to integrating your body and mind. Getting back into your body is such an important aspect of living— you need to live *inside* you, not constantly on the run from your traumas and the past. Listen to your body; hear what it has to tell you. It knows all your traumas and triggers, and now, you can respond to its needs by simply referring to the ChakraMents. If this means you need to heal, grow, gain awareness, move, or whatever it is you need to do to get back into your body, do it. To make an impact in the present, you need to *live* in the present. Rely on yourself to overcome the odds. Channel the elements within you to help you thrive and rise to your highest potential. And rely on your resources—this book, your support network, yourself—to keep you on the path to peace and growth.

Trust your own inner knowledge. Everything you need to make the next step already exists inside of your body. The answers are there. You just need the self-love and confidence to listen.

This is it. You have a model in your hands now, a methodology to make sense of yourself. Dive into the ChakraMent system. Share it with your loved ones so you can uplift each other. Begin speaking the same element-focused language with them, using the ChakraMental Method™ to explain your feelings and understand each other in new ways. Use the movement exercises detailed in the chapters—maybe even host a self-care party where you and all your friends can play the different elemental songs on the stereo and groove to them.

Working on yourself can be fulfilling and enlightening. Just remember to have fun with it!

ACKNOWLEDGMENTS

I have to start by thanking my mother, Sue, who believed in me no matter what. She recognized me as a wild spirit and cultivated my confidence throughout my life.

To Rick, thank you for being my guardian and my "guard rails." Because of you, I have been able to focus, finish this book, and find the peace inside me you always knew was there.

To my fierce friend India, thank you for your loving, no-frills honesty. You have gently pulled me back from my shadow and helped me connect with my soul.

To my team at BrightRay Publishing, especially Arya and Jamie, who pulled out my stories with wonder and enthusiasm—you have been a dream to work with.

To the goddesses, Molly, Deanna, Rosie, and Toni, who know all of me and still love me—thank you all for always pushing me to be the best version of myself. Thank you for being my sounding board, my confidants, and my friends.

 **APPENDIX**

FOOD CRAVINGS, CHAKRAMENTS, AND WHAT THEY MEAN

Lacking a ChakraMent?	You May Need to Eat . . .

Earth
 	
1st Chakra: Root
	■ Farm-to-table foods
	  ◆ Root vegetables like carrots and potatoes
	  ◆ Meats, such as ground beef
	  ◆ Grains

Water
 	
2nd Chakra:
Below the belly button
	■ Hydrating foods
	  ◆ Coconut water
	  ◆ Watery fruits and vegetables
	  ◆ Yogurt

Wood
 	
3rd Chakra: Solar plexus
	■ Vitamins and minerals
	  ◆ Calcium
	  ◆ Magnesium
	■ Salty, crispy, and crunchy snacks
	  ◆ Potato chips

Fire
 	
4th Chakra: Heart
	■ Spicy foods
	  ◆ Hot sauce
	  ◆ Peppers
	  ◆ Curry

Air
 	
5th Chakra: Throat
	■ Light and airy foods
	  ◆ Whipped Cream
	  ◆ Marshmallows
	  ◆ Honey

Metal 6th Chakra: Third eye	<ul><li>Clean, nourishing foods<ul><li>Raw fruits and vegetables</li><li>Berries</li><li>Nuts</li></ul></li></ul>
Ether 7th Chakra: Crown	<ul><li>Dopamine-inducing foods<ul><li>Dark chocolate</li></ul></li><li>"Soul" foods<ul><li>Other ways of taking in nutrients, such as gaining vitamin D from sunshine, therapeutic heat and massage, and breath work</li></ul></li></ul>

THE CHAKRAMENT VOWEL SOUNDS

Meditate by repeatedly chanting these vowel sounds, either out loud or in your inner mind, to strengthen the desired ChakraMent.

ChakraMent	Vowel Sound
Earth 1st Chakra: Root	"*Uh*" as in pup
Water 2nd Chakra: Below the belly button	"*Ooo*" as in soon
Wood 3rd Chakra: Solar plexus	"*Oh*" as in know
Fire 4th Chakra: Heart	"*Ah*" as in spa
Air 5th Chakra: Throat	"*Eye*" as in why
Metal 6th Chakra: Third eye	"*Aaa*" as in lay
Ether 7th Chakra: Crown	"*Eee*" as in see

CHAKRAMENT RESOURCES AND LINKS

Earth

Earth Spotify Playlist:

Self-Reflection Questions	Symptoms of Disconnect	Affirmations
■ Do I feel grounded? ■ Do I encourage and support myself? ■ Am I supported by my family, community, and friends?	■ Fatigue and sluggishness ■ Constipation or diarrhea ■ Uneasiness in your body ■ Feeling anxious, insecure, unstable, and shaky ■ Experiencing chronic depression	■ I trust myself. ■ I listen to my body and its messages. ■ My unique way to rebound builds confidence and self-respect. ■ Mother Earth will always be there for me. Whenever I need to collect myself, I connect to her soil.

Earth: Movement Exercise

To understand how connection with the earth feels, let's do a quick grounding exercise that will help you embrace three important aspects—the earth element, the root chakra, and yourself.

Sit comfortably on the ground with your legs crossed. Close your eyes. Feel your sitz bones sink into the earth, and begin to relax the body. Ask your joints to release any pain and become aware of your spine. Notice how your head is balanced on your neck, and let your thoughts spill down your spine through your tailbone and into the earth.

Let your tailbone root in the dark earth, and imagine it holding you upright, supporting the entire weight of your body. Now, you are rooted deep in the soil like the roots of a tree, so you can never waver, never shake. But you can sit still in peace, trusting the earth to hold you in place. It anchors your body and your mind, fostering deep confidence and peace.

Give in. Surrender your anxieties, worries, and burdens. Send them down deep into the ground through your spine. The earth will absorb your burdens, just as a mother would. Rely on your courage, fearlessness, and self-assurance to help you bounce back. Rebound as high as you can, knowing that even if you fall, you will never fail because the earth, your ultimate safety net, will receive you.

Earth: Grounding Meditation

This earth exercise can be done at your personal pace and needs. It's particularly great to do as a start-of-the-day meditation or as a way to get grounded and clear the head in any situation.

Stand on the ground, preferably barefoot in the earth, but this can be done just fine with shoes on concrete.

Close your eyes slightly or all the way. Feel your feet: your heels, the sides, and the padding in front. Wiggle your toes, and drum them on the floor.

From between your big toe and second toe, grow a root down through the floor into the earth below. Keep growing your roots, past the rocks and shale, and deep into the center of the earth into the molten, fiery, energetic center. Let your roots become straws to suck up this energy, and draw it back up into your feet. Feel it energize all the bones and muscles in your feet, those things that support you as you move.

Draw this energy up the ankles, and feel this give lift to your joints there. Now, move it up your shins and calves into your knees, and again, feel the space it brings to your knee joints. Continue moving it up to your thighs, the large muscles that move your body from one location to the next. Feel your thighs burn with energy as it passes into your hip joints, lubricating this area to roll and release when you walk.

Allow this energy to migrate into your lower belly, the dantian, where nurturing your sensuality happens. This is your creative center, so notice how it ignites. Feel the energy wash over your stomach and soothe any discomfort there. As it rises into your chest, let it kindle your heart, your passion, and your desires.

Take a deep breath into your lungs, and pull this lovely energy up and over your shoulders. Let it fall down your arms like water and stream off your shoulders like a waterfall, taking with it all the "should"s and the weight of your worries. As the energy moves to the throat, let it clear any blocks to you speaking your heart. Clear your throat. As this energy makes it up through your face, let it melt any tension in your jaw or forehead. And when it reaches the top, open your crown chakra, and let it out to connect with the divine.

There. Now you have connected heaven and earth. Your body is the conduit for both.

Water

Water Spotify Playlist:

Self-Reflection Questions	Symptoms of Disconnect	Affirmations
- Am I inflexible? - Am I rigid, non-negotiable, or uncoachable? - Where am I stuck or blocked? Have I hit an impasse? - Do I have fears about money or the lack of money? - Do I feel sensual and sexy in my body? - Am I comfortable connecting with others? - Am I wishy-washy? - Do I have no direction?	- Uterine cysts - Chronic bladder issues - Kidney stones - Painful sex and lack of sensuality - Lower back pain - Feeling "stuck" - Indecisiveness - Feeling overwhelmed, anxious, and stressed	- I am adaptable. - I am creative in my flexibility. - I have the ability to flow and self-sooth. - I embrace all of me—the good, bad, beautiful, and challenging—with grace. - I am gentle with myself.

■ Do I lack the motivation to move forward in my life?		

Water: Movement Exercise

Water is a connected flow. From trickle to stream to river to ocean, it will find a way.

Put on some music that is flowy, sexy, sensual, feminine, and syrupy. Imagine diving into a vat of honey. Suspended, swimming, feel your body as one organism, not just a bunch of parts put together.

Start by swaying your hips. Then, include your thighs, moving them in a circular motion and connecting the bones in a watery movement as with a mermaid's tail. Bring this sensual movement into the mid-belly and your ribs, moving your spine like a snake. Soften your shoulders and shrug off the "should"s, letting them melt and roll down your arms like water. Move your arms like big paintbrushes, painting the world around you. Then, bring all this flexibility up into the neck, rolling your head and feeling any stiffness or pain. Think about what is upsetting you—keep moving, swaying, circling, engulfing this feeling in your movement. Ask what it is and what it needs. Dislodge it and let it flow with your movements. Whatever you do, don't stop—keep flowing through the intensity of your emotions. This could be expressed as tears or anger, or maybe you just need to wrap your arms around yourself in a hug.

Keep moving. Let your body tell the story of what you are feeling. I have observed in most clients that underneath anger is sadness, and once the anger is expressed, sometimes the real root of sadness shows up. Keep moving even when you want to stop.

Move with your feelings.

Let them be there.

Let them be okay.

You are okay.

Water: Creative Flow Exercise

If you're a writer, painter, dancer, or any creative experiencing a block, I challenge you. Put on some music that is sexy and central to you (something you deeply resonate with), slightly close your eyes, and focus internally. Begin to move. Sway with the music; let it move every part of your body like it is the blood nourishing it. Just move. No other directions.

You feel like moving your hips? Do it.

You feel shaking your head to the rhythm? Do it.

Want to jump up and down? Spin in circles? Move like a fish? Do it. Do it. Do it.

Think about softening all your joints and trying to move your body in ways you haven't done before. Sink your head into those visions entirely. Forget about your art. Forget your deadlines. Forget any anxiety you may have about other people's opinions. Empty your head.

Do this for the whole piece of music.

Feeling a little more relaxed?

Now, allow your art to flow without restrictions and judgment. Let it just flow out of you. No thoughts about form or structure or requirements. Allow the *flow* to take you where it needs to *go*. Your fear about fulfilling expectations and performing well—they're all slowing you down, blocking you. Let all these thoughts out. All you're doing now is channeling your artistic abilities, flowing freely, and creating unbelievable and important things.

You are water. Do you see how beautiful that is?

Wood

Wood Spotify Playlist:

Self-Reflection Questions	Symptoms of Disconnect	Affirmations
<ul><li>Do I support myself?</li><li>Do I find humor in the silver linings?</li><li>Do I believe in myself unconditionally?</li><li>Do I stand up for myself?</li><li>Do I recognize what needs to go and release it?</li></ul>	<ul><li>Irritable Bowel Syndrome (IBS)</li><li>Abnormal/ excessive weight gain or loss</li><li>Ulcers</li><li>Diabetes</li><li>Issues in pancreas, liver, or colon</li><li>Heartburn</li><li>Eating disorders</li><li>Low self-esteem and confidence</li></ul>	<ul><li>I am amused by myself.</li><li>I shake off my negative thoughts and feelings.</li><li>My self-doubt drops like dead leaves in the fall.</li><li>I let go of the "should"s weighing on my shoulders.</li><li>I delight in myself.</li></ul>

Wood: Movement Exercise

Put this music on:

Let your head bob with this quirky, staccato, piano piece from Charlie Brown and your childhood. Take the head bob into your shoulders and let your shoulders and arms dance in non-syncopated, playful movements. Shrug off any stiffness, pain, and "should"s. Let your chest, waist, and hips bounce like an excited child. As you trickle down this rhythm (arrhythmia!) to your legs, separate the bones on the way down to your feet. Pretend you are on hot sand, and pick your feet up and down rapidly so they won't get burned. Let yourself laugh at your own silliness—I mean, belly laugh! Now, how do you feel?

Fire

Fire Spotify Playlist:

Self-Reflection Questions	Symptoms of Disconnect	Affirmations
▪ Do I love myself? ▪ Am I connected to my desires and passions? ▪ Do I feel like I am one big hot button? ▪ Am I motivated?	▪ High temperature and flushing red in the face or parts of the body ▪ Feeling dehydrated all the time ▪ Dry, flaky skin ▪ Heartburn and high blood pressure ▪ Feeling perpetually angry and ready to explode with very little triggering, or feeling apathetic and lethargic	▪ I am passionate about my dreams and pursuits. ▪ My desires drive me. ▪ I connect to the rhythm of life.

	<ul><li>Feeling routinely stressed</li><li>Uncontrollably driven or lack of drive</li><li>Feeling cold all the time and clammy hands</li><li>Lung and breathing issues</li><li>Inability to express compassion</li></ul>	

Fire: Compassion Meditation Exercise

Close your eyes, and picture someone you absolutely detest. Someone who fans the flames of your anger. The feeling can be so intense that it makes you want to take action just to relieve the steam building up within you like a pressure cooker. It is at this moment that alchemical redirection can happen.

Admit that your greatest desire is to have peace in your heart and not a burning hatred. The path to peace is compassion. Again, put space between you and this person and their actions, and look at them from a different perspective. Think about how horrible they must feel about themselves to project such appalling behavior toward you. This perspective takes you out of the equation and gives the piss and vinegar back to them. Sometimes, "the only winning move is not to play."[3] Truly happy people don't do dreadful things to others. The greater the scale of the horrendous behavior, the greater their inner war is. It's not easy; believe me, I know. But still, I urge you to find a crumb of mercy because, when you do this, you convert that angry fire to compassion, even pity, and you can walk away with no attachment to that person or their actions. You feel so much lighter. You gain control.

Air

Air Spotify Playlist:

Self-Reflection Questions	Symptoms of Disconnect	Affirmations
■ Am I being truthful with myself? ■ Am I speaking my truth to others? ■ What am I not expressing? ■ Where am I oppressed?	■ Feeling a lump in your throat or overwhelming emotions ■ Difficulty in breathing or tightness in the lungs ■ Desire to smoke tobacco and cannabis (to suppress grief situated in the lungs) ■ Cough and a build-up of phlegm ■ Chronic lung and throat issues ■ Low, resigned voice (like Eeyore)	■ I am the messenger. ■ I am needed. ■ My gifts are destined. ■ I am unique and deserve expression. ■ To not express what I truly feel or can do is hiding my God-given gifts from everyone.

	■ Feeling physically "deflated" or emotionally "lifeless"	
	■ Feeling helpless, restricted, or incarcerated as if you have no control over your own life	
	■ Reacting defensively to most situations	

Air: Emotional Clarity Exercise

Partner up with someone, and ask them to place one hand on your upper back, against the fourth chakra (your heart), and another hand on your mid-back, near the third chakra (your solar plexus). Start speaking. Talk about something that is weighing on your mind, and feel the vibrations where your partner has placed their hands. Feel and hear the difference in your voice when your emotions emerge from these areas that are supported.

Now that you know what this feels like, try to replicate these feelings the next time you try to communicate your feelings to someone else. Reflect on how calm the feeling makes you, how it prepares you to first create a safe space, and then calmly express your thoughts and emotions.

Project your voice without straining it.

Direct all the energy from deep in your body, all the way up and out, and not just from your throat.

Feel the sound of your voice and emotions through your entire body, like air rushing through you.

By grounding yourself this way, you can prevent yourself from expressing the *wrong* way. You won't spiral into spewing hate onto someone else or violently attacking them. Instead, you'll be able to be objective, express it all out into the air, and take it from there.

Metal

Metal Spotify Playlist:

Self-Reflection Questions	Symptoms of Disconnect	Affirmations
<ul><li>What are my goals?</li><li>How am I distracted? What is my remedy?</li><li>What is my "why"?</li><li>Why do I lack focus?</li><li>How do I feel whenever I make progress?</li><li>Why do I let people or situations stand in my way?</li><li>What am I committed to?</li><li>How will I support my determination?</li></ul>	<ul><li>Indecisiveness and lack of opinions</li><li>Feeling "lost" or directionless</li><li>A negative outlook on life and self</li><li>Fear of commitment</li><li>Easily distracted or the inability to focus</li><li>Foggy brain</li></ul>	<ul><li>I know what I want.</li><li>I can say no to distraction.</li><li>I can stay focused.</li><li>I have my goals in focus.</li><li>I practice intentional discipline.</li></ul>

Metal: Self-Reflection Exercise

Like with all elements, metal starts with your breath. To reach discernment, you must first distance yourself from the chaos of human life. Turn everything off—your phone, the TV, the lights—and shut the door. Let everything around you become quiet so all you can hear is the faint sound of your own breathing. Check your distractions at the door, whether they be work stress, relationship issues, or health problems. From here on out, all you should focus on is allowing a higher plane of existence from where you can see and sense *everything*. This is the best time to let in the loftiest of thoughts, those that may even seem unattainable, into your vision.

What are your relationship, health, career, or family goals?

What's your "why" for each?

What has worked in the past?

What hasn't? (These are your distractions and course destroyers.)

Walk back from these goals and set attainable benchmarks—steps that get you closer to your goals. Write all this down and set up reminders of the benchmarks on your calendar. Celebrate each accomplishment toward your goals, no matter how small. The movement is forward and onward!

Metal: "A Day in the Life" Meditation Exercise

"A Day in the Life" is one of my most-used active meditations that I guide my clients through, especially when they are in desperate need of some metal in their lives. I ask them to gently close their eyes and quiet their internal distractions.

Then, I slowly ask them reflection questions about what their life may look like five years from now:

- As you wake up in the morning, what does your bed feel like?
- Look out of the window in your room. What do you see outside? Where are you living?
- Take stock of your body. How does it feel?
- What do you do next?
- What do you have on your agenda for the day?
- Who do you meet and talk to?
- How do you end your day?
- What have you achieved? What are you still working on?

With every question, I guide my clients to dig in deep and be specific. Five years from now, one of them might look out their window and see downtown New York while others might see a forest. They may take stock of their body and feel physically fit, energetic, their ideal body weight. Their plans for the day might include meeting with the CEO of a company that they've always wanted to partner with or going on a date with someone who looks like their dream version of a partner. They might end their day feeling satisfied and grateful, maybe sharing a glass of wine with a loved one. Visioning is powerful. This is the time to let your imagination go wild with no restrictions or attention to roadblocks. What influences your dream the most are your emotions. In this exercise, allow the smells, tastes, visuals, and feelings to get specific and intense. They are the lighthouses for your visions, beckoning your dreams into reality.

The situations vary for each person, of course, but they all have one similarity: what they imagine five years from now is their "why." Whether they knew about it before the meditation or not, what they visualized was their reason for waking up every morning. Once the meditation clarifies your world for you, your direction and immediate next steps become apparent. Channel the metal element—feel the determination and focus direct you.

Set your eyes on the horizon, and start your journey.

Ether Spotify Playlist:

Self-Reflection Questions	Symptoms of Disconnect	Affirmations
<ul><li>Where do I feel the calmest and most comfortable?</li><li>What would I call my sanctuary or sacred space?</li><li>What does my gentle inner voice sound like?</li><li>Where am I able to breathe and connect with nature?</li><li>Can I quiet my mind, or do I need help?</li><li>Do I believe in a greater universe, a higher power, or an omnipotent and loving energy?</li></ul>	<ul><li>Having a hunched-over posture</li><li>Avoiding eye contact or even physically avoiding people</li><li>Constantly in a state of worry and anxiety</li><li>Experiencing melancholy, grief, or guilt</li><li>Feeling defeated or joyless</li></ul>	<ul><li>I am connected to my highest purpose.</li><li>I am integrated, and my message transcends.</li><li>I hear the universe's messages.</li><li>I embrace all of me unconditionally.</li></ul>

■ Do I have radical acceptance of myself?		

Ether: Gratitude Meditation Exercise

Find a quiet peaceful place, whether inside or out. Make sure there will be no interruptions—phone calls, electronic notifications, or external annoyances such as sirens or traffic. Get comfortable. You can either stand or sit for this exercise.

Make sure you are in your body by wiggling your toes and squeezing the muscles in each section of your body like flexing your thighs and then letting them relax. Start with your toes, and do this all the way up to the top of your head. When you get to your face, clench your jaws first and then let them relax. Gently close your eyes partially or all the way. Now, imagine your forehead melting like chocolate streaming down your cheeks and jaw, taking any tension with it. Imagine the top of your head and notice any sensations there. This is where you can connect to the pineal gland residing in the middle of your brain, a mood regulator in concert with the limbic system. There is another gland here in the middle called the amygdala. This is the "gatekeeper" between your primal brain stem and the cerebral cortex, and it is responsible for consequential thinking (in other words, it weighs the costs and benefits of your choices). Your amygdala is important as it allows you to pause, evaluate, and respond to make better decisions. Imagine a golden gate between the top of your head and a brightly lit path upwards to the heavens, the universe. Connect this to your higher self, god, goddess, and your guides, who are here to help you.

Breathe in slowly for four to eight counts and exhale for four to eight counts. Following your breath, shut out the chatter in your brain with a calming mantra—one as simple as "I breathe in love, and I exhale stress and anger."

Repeat this again and again as you open the golden gate at the top of your head and let in the beam of light. Allow it to fill you up and make its way to tiny dark places, crevices that you may not have noticed before. Let it open up the closed and sheltered parts of you and shine its loving light into the shadows present. When we slow down enough, sometimes the negative dark aspect of ourselves (the "shadow") seeps up into our mind. But this is when you have an opportunity to surround your body with love as if it were a crying baby. Embrace this hurt part of you, let it be present without judgment, and shift your attention to someone you love. Feel your joy in the moment.

Ether is about allowing it *all* to exist at the same time. As you feel and observe your emotions, marvel at the complexity and intricacy that make you unique. As scenes and feelings flow in and out of your focus, imagine them as individual threads of different colors weaving the beautiful tapestry of your life. You may hug yourself, or sway gently, or raise your arms and float in a nurturing way. Let this lightness bring levity to all your feelings. Let them rise up like clouds. Just *float*. Imagine yourself suspended in the clouds, in space. Listen . . . this is when you can receive messages that otherwise can't get through the cacophony of life. If there is a nagging thought, put it in a balloon, seal it off, and let it float away until it disappears. Stay here as long as you can.

Before you close out this moment and move on, give yourself gratitude for all of the feelings that have been revealed. Give your body gratitude for slowing down enough to be in suspension. Give your mind love for choosing to give yourself this moment. Finally, thank your heart for all it has endured and how it has communicated with you. Bask in your own gratitude, and then slowly open your eyes and move back into your day.

 **NOTES**

Introduction

1. Maureen Salamon, "What Is Somatic Therapy?" *Harvard Health Publishing* (blog), Harvard Medical School, July 7, 2023, https://www. health.harvard.edu/blog/what-is-somatic-therapy-202307072951.

2. "The Dance of Yoga, the Yoga of Dance," Kripalu Center for Yoga and Health, accessed July 3, 2024, https://kripalu.org/resources/dance-yoga-yoga-dance.

Chapter One

1. Allan Schore, "Paradigm Shift: The Right Brain and the Relational Unconscious," (January 2008): https://www.researchgate.net/publication/252303085_paradigm_shift_the_right_brain_and_the_relational_unconscious.

2. Brianna Chu, Komal Marwaha, Terrence Sanvictores, Ayoola O. Awosika, and Derek Ayers, *Physiology, Stress Reaction* (Treasure Island, FL: StatPearls Publishing, 2022).

3. Bsaikrishna, "Fear the Root of Anger, Sadness, Anxiety, and Guilt," *Brandalyzer* (blog), June 10, 2019, https://brandalyzer.blog/2019/06/10/fear-the-root-of-anger-sadness-and-anxiety/.

4. Sarah Warren, "What Is Somatic Movement?" Somatic Movement Center, January 5, 2016, https://somaticmovementcenter.com/somatic-movement-what-is-somatic-movement/.

5. Zawn Villines, "What Are Chakras and How Do They Affect Health?" Medical News Today, updated November 20, 2023, https://www.medicalnewstoday.com/articles/what-are-chakras-concept-origins-and-effect-on-health.

6. Sharon Begley, *Train Your Mind, Change Your Brain: How a New Science Reveals Our Extraordinary Potential to Transform Ourselves* (New York: Ballantine Books, 2007).

Chapter Two

1. "Social Anxiety Disorder," Mental Health America, accessed July 3, 2024, https://www.mhanational.org/conditions/social-anxiety-disorder.

2. Ashton Clarke, "Muscle Testing. Is It Legit?" Healthline, November 29, 2018, https://www.healthline.com/health/muscle-testing.

Chapter Three

1. Alex Rennie, "Emotional Men: Do Women Prefer a Man Who Can Cry?" Elite Singles, accessed July 3, 2024, https://www.elitesingles.com/mag/relationship-advice/emotional-men.

Chapter Four

1. "Exercising to Relax," *Harvard Health Publishing* (blog), Harvard Medical School, July 7, 2020, https://www.health.harvard.edu/staying-healthy/exercising-to-relax.

2. "Concept of Rasa – An Ayurvedic Guide for Yogis," Samyak Institute of Yoga & Ayurveda, March 11, 2022, https://www.samyakyoga.org/ https-www-samyakyoga-org-concept-of-rasa-an-ayurvedic-guide-for-yogis.

3. "Craving Salt: What It Means and What You Can Do About It?" The Ayurveda Experience, August 1, 2023, https://theayurvedaexperience.com/blogs/tae/craving-salt-what-it-means-what-you-can-do.

Chapter Five

1. "Everything You Need to Know About the Heart Chakra," Yoga Journal, updated April 24, 2023, https://www.yogajournal.com/yoga-101/chakras-yoga-for-beginners/intro-heart-chakra-anahata/.

2. "What Is The Meaning of Anahata Chakra?" The Yogic Encyclopedia, Ananda, https://www.ananda.org/yogapedia/anahata-chakra/.

3. *Wargames*, directed by John Badham (United States: MGM/UA Entertainment Company, 1983). This line was spoken by Joshua (voiced by John Wood).

Chapter Six

1. Bernard Golden, "Fear and Anger: Similarities, Differences, and Interaction," Psychology Today, March 20, 2021, https://www.psychologytoday.com/us/blog/overcoming-destructive-anger/202103/fear-and-anger-similarities-differences-and-interaction.

2. Louise Hay, *Heal Your Body* (Carlsbad, CA: Hay House Publishing, 1984).

3. "Nrityagram," Nrityagram Dance Village, accessed July 3, 2024, https://nrityagram.org/.

4. "Vision," Nrityagram Dance Village, accessed July 3, 2024, https://nrityagram.org/vision.

5. "Level 1 Kirtan Training," Kirtan Leader Institute, accessed July 3, 2024, https://www.kirtanleader.com/kli-level-1.

Chapter Seven

1. Alex Nash, "The Akashic Records: Origins and Relation to Western Concepts," *Central European Journal of Contemporary Religion* 3, no. 2 (2019): 109–124, https://doi.org/10.14712/25704893.2020.3.

Chapter Eight

1. "Alex Grey," Alex Grey, accessed July 3, 2024, https://www.alexgrey.com/.

2. India Prema, *Burning Down the House: Transforming Yourself Into a Powerful New Life* (Sedona, AZ: Warrior Spirit, 2023).

3. "Ananda Marga," Ananda Marga, accessed July 3, 2024, https://www.anandamarga.org/.

ABOUT THE AUTHOR

Angel Howard is a certified somatic movement therapist who has held a myriad of titles: executive coach, retreat host, inspirational speaker, professional dancer and choreographer, holistic healer, published writer, and TV and radio show host, among others. Her organization, WildHeart Expressive, is a somatic movement and dance retreat program that empowers others to release stuck traumas, facilitate change in habits and beliefs, and bring joy to everyday living.

Angel has had a heightened connection to her body since childhood. High school cheerleading and professional dance performances taught her to trust her body. Corporate positions at companies such as Coca-Cola, Atlanta Financial Group, and the Legacy Housing Foundation only developed that innate connection further by teaching her the importance of body language and expression in interpersonal relationships. Then, later, as the executive director of a river protection and preservation organization, she discovered that her inner confidence in body and spirit propelled her to achieve action for a cause.

Since attending the Omega Institute and receiving her certification in 1999, Angel has seen somatic therapy movement as the perfect marriage between her psychology and dance training. Now, with more than 25 years of experience, she has cultivated a platform for self-discovery and unlocking one's truest potential through body acceptance and love. WildHeart Expressive has grown into a global community that enables people to find their passions, create self-love rituals, unearth their unique voices, and practice courage and confidence in every step forward.

Angel earned her bachelor's in psychology from Hollins University and an international master's degree in business and finance from the University of Monaco. She continues to participate in various private organizations, nonprofits, and boards, including the Women's Fund of East Tennessee, the Knoxville Symphony, Women in Entrepreneurship, and Let Her Speak. She lives in her hometown of Knoxville, Tennessee, with her partner, Rick, and two entertaining Havanese pups—Gypsy and Frank.

Made in the USA
Columbia, SC
26 September 2024

43077263R10124